C-1932 CAREER EXAMINATION SERIES

This is your
PASSBOOK for...

Principal Library Clerk

Test Preparation Study Guide
Questions & Answers

COPYRIGHT NOTICE

This book is SOLELY intended for, is sold ONLY to, and its use is RESTRICTED to individual, bona fide applicants or candidates who qualify by virtue of having seriously filed applications for appropriate license, certificate, professional and/or promotional advancement, higher school matriculation, scholarship, or other legitimate requirements of education and/or governmental authorities.

This book is NOT intended for use, class instruction, tutoring, training, duplication, copying, reprinting, excerption, or adaptation, etc., by:

1) Other publishers
2) Proprietors and/or Instructors of "Coaching" and/or Preparatory Courses
3) Personnel and/or Training Divisions of commercial, industrial, and governmental organizations
4) Schools, colleges, or universities and/or their departments and staffs, including teachers and other personnel
5) Testing Agencies or Bureaus
6) Study groups which seek by the purchase of a single volume to copy and/or duplicate and/or adapt this material for use by the group as a whole without having purchased individual volumes for each of the members of the group
7) Et al.

Such persons would be in violation of appropriate Federal and State statutes.

PROVISION OF LICENSING AGREEMENTS – Recognized educational, commercial, industrial, and governmental institutions and organizations, and others legitimately engaged in educational pursuits, including training, testing, and measurement activities, may address request for a licensing agreement to the copyright owners, who will determine whether, and under what conditions, including fees and charges, the materials in this book may be used them. In other words, a licensing facility exists for the legitimate use of the material in this book on other than an individual basis. However, it is asseverated and affirmed here that the material in this book CANNOT be used without the receipt of the express permission of such a licensing agreement from the Publishers. Inquiries re licensing should be addressed to the company, attention rights and permissions department.

All rights reserved, including the right of reproduction in whole or in part, in any form or by any means, electronic or mechanical, including photocopying, recording, or by any information storage and retrieval system, without permission in writing from the Publisher.

Copyright © 2023 by
National Learning Corporation

212 Michael Drive, Syosset, NY 11791
(516) 921-8888 • www.passbooks.com
E-mail: info@passbooks.com

PUBLISHED IN THE UNITED STATES OF AMERICA

PASSBOOK® SERIES

THE *PASSBOOK® SERIES* has been created to prepare applicants and candidates for the ultimate academic battlefield – the examination room.

At some time in our lives, each and every one of us may be required to take an examination – for validation, matriculation, admission, qualification, registration, certification, or licensure.

Based on the assumption that every applicant or candidate has met the basic formal educational standards, has taken the required number of courses, and read the necessary texts, the *PASSBOOK® SERIES* furnishes the one special preparation which may assure passing with confidence, instead of failing with insecurity. Examination questions – together with answers – are furnished as the basic vehicle for study so that the mysteries of the examination and its compounding difficulties may be eliminated or diminished by a sure method.

This book is meant to help you pass your examination provided that you qualify and are serious in your objective.

The entire field is reviewed through the huge store of content information which is succinctly presented through a provocative and challenging approach – the question-and-answer method.

A climate of success is established by furnishing the correct answers at the end of each test.

You soon learn to recognize types of questions, forms of questions, and patterns of questioning. You may even begin to anticipate expected outcomes.

You perceive that many questions are repeated or adapted so that you can gain acute insights, which may enable you to score many sure points.

You learn how to confront new questions, or types of questions, and to attack them confidently and work out the correct answers.

You note objectives and emphases, and recognize pitfalls and dangers, so that you may make positive educational adjustments.

Moreover, you are kept fully informed in relation to new concepts, methods, practices, and directions in the field.

You discover that you are actually taking the examination all the time: you are preparing for the examination by "taking" an examination, not by reading extraneous and/or supererogatory textbooks.

In short, this PASSBOOK®, used directedly, should be an important factor in helping you to pass your test.

PRINCIPAL LIBRARY CLERK

DUTIES

Assists a Librarian in charging and discharging books registering, borrowers, collecting fines, reserving books and answering the more difficult questions concerning the library's collections and services while working at the circulation and reference desks. Supervises the preparation of overdue notices, catalog cards and filing of shelf list cards; oversees and revises the pasting and lettering of new books; prepares books and magazines for the bindery. Supervises the maintenance of records and assists in the preparation of bills, purchase orders, payroll and statistical reports for the main and branch libraries.

Under the general supervision of a Librarian, Library Director, or Library Media Specialist, incumbents supervise and perform specialized clerical work requiring advanced knowledge of library techniques and routines. An incumbent receives general instructions and then plans, assigns and reviews the work of other clerical employees. This class differs from that of Senior Library Clerk in that incumbents exercise a greater degree of independent judgement and decision making, with wide discretion for planning and carrying out assignments. Incumbents may be responsible for several functional units of a library, i.e., circulation, technical services, etc., and may participate in performing duties assigned to subordinates. Supervision is exercised over Senior Library Clerks, Library Clerks, Pages, and volunteers. Does related work as required

SCOPE OF THE EXAMINATION

The written test is designed to test for knowledge, skills, and/or abilities in such areas as:
1. Fundamentals of working in a library;
2. Name and number checking;
3. Office record keeping;
4. Public contact principles and practices; and
5. Supervision.

HOW TO TAKE A TEST

I. YOU MUST PASS AN EXAMINATION

A. *WHAT EVERY CANDIDATE SHOULD KNOW*

Examination applicants often ask us for help in preparing for the written test. What can I study in advance? What kinds of questions will be asked? How will the test be given? How will the papers be graded?

As an applicant for a civil service examination, you may be wondering about some of these things. Our purpose here is to suggest effective methods of advance study and to describe civil service examinations.

Your chances for success on this examination can be increased if you know how to prepare. Those "pre-examination jitters" can be reduced if you know what to expect. You can even experience an adventure in good citizenship if you know why civil service exams are given.

B. *WHY ARE CIVIL SERVICE EXAMINATIONS GIVEN?*

Civil service examinations are important to you in two ways. As a citizen, you want public jobs filled by employees who know how to do their work. As a job seeker, you want a fair chance to compete for that job on an equal footing with other candidates. The best-known means of accomplishing this two-fold goal is the competitive examination.

Exams are widely publicized throughout the nation. They may be administered for jobs in federal, state, city, municipal, town or village governments or agencies.

Any citizen may apply, with some limitations, such as the age or residence of applicants. Your experience and education may be reviewed to see whether you meet the requirements for the particular examination. When these requirements exist, they are reasonable and applied consistently to all applicants. Thus, a competitive examination may cause you some uneasiness now, but it is your privilege and safeguard.

C. *HOW ARE CIVIL SERVICE EXAMS DEVELOPED?*

Examinations are carefully written by trained technicians who are specialists in the field known as "psychological measurement," in consultation with recognized authorities in the field of work that the test will cover. These experts recommend the subject matter areas or skills to be tested; only those knowledges or skills important to your success on the job are included. The most reliable books and source materials available are used as references. Together, the experts and technicians judge the difficulty level of the questions.

Test technicians know how to phrase questions so that the problem is clearly stated. Their ethics do not permit "trick" or "catch" questions. Questions may have been tried out on sample groups, or subjected to statistical analysis, to determine their usefulness.

Written tests are often used in combination with performance tests, ratings of training and experience, and oral interviews. All of these measures combine to form the best-known means of finding the right person for the right job.

II. HOW TO PASS THE WRITTEN TEST

A. NATURE OF THE EXAMINATION

To prepare intelligently for civil service examinations, you should know how they differ from school examinations you have taken. In school you were assigned certain definite pages to read or subjects to cover. The examination questions were quite detailed and usually emphasized memory. Civil service exams, on the other hand, try to discover your present ability to perform the duties of a position, plus your potentiality to learn these duties. In other words, a civil service exam attempts to predict how successful you will be. Questions cover such a broad area that they cannot be as minute and detailed as school exam questions.

In the public service similar kinds of work, or positions, are grouped together in one "class." This process is known as *position-classification*. All the positions in a class are paid according to the salary range for that class. One class title covers all of these positions, and they are all tested by the same examination.

B. FOUR BASIC STEPS

1) Study the announcement

How, then, can you know what subjects to study? Our best answer is: "Learn as much as possible about the class of positions for which you've applied." The exam will test the knowledge, skills and abilities needed to do the work.

Your most valuable source of information about the position you want is the official exam announcement. This announcement lists the training and experience qualifications. Check these standards and apply only if you come reasonably close to meeting them.

The brief description of the position in the examination announcement offers some clues to the subjects which will be tested. Think about the job itself. Review the duties in your mind. Can you perform them, or are there some in which you are rusty? Fill in the blank spots in your preparation.

Many jurisdictions preview the written test in the exam announcement by including a section called "Knowledge and Abilities Required," "Scope of the Examination," or some similar heading. Here you will find out specifically what fields will be tested.

2) Review your own background

Once you learn in general what the position is all about, and what you need to know to do the work, ask yourself which subjects you already know fairly well and which need improvement. You may wonder whether to concentrate on improving your strong areas or on building some background in your fields of weakness. When the announcement has specified "some knowledge" or "considerable knowledge," or has used adjectives like "beginning principles of..." or "advanced ... methods," you can get a clue as to the number and difficulty of questions to be asked in any given field. More questions, and hence broader coverage, would be included for those subjects which are more important in the work. Now weigh your strengths and weaknesses against the job requirements and prepare accordingly.

3) Determine the level of the position

Another way to tell how intensively you should prepare is to understand the level of the job for which you are applying. Is it the entering level? In other words, is this the position in which beginners in a field of work are hired? Or is it an intermediate or advanced level? Sometimes this is indicated by such words as "Junior" or "Senior" in the class title. Other jurisdictions use Roman numerals to designate the level – Clerk I, Clerk II, for example. The word "Supervisor" sometimes appears in the title. If the level is not indicated by the title, check the description of duties. Will you be working under very close supervision, or will you have responsibility for independent decisions in this work?

4) Choose appropriate study materials

Now that you know the subjects to be examined and the relative amount of each subject to be covered, you can choose suitable study materials. For beginning level jobs, or even advanced ones, if you have a pronounced weakness in some aspect of your training, read a modern, standard textbook in that field. Be sure it is up to date and has general coverage. Such books are normally available at your library, and the librarian will be glad to help you locate one. For entry-level positions, questions of appropriate difficulty are chosen – neither highly advanced questions, nor those too simple. Such questions require careful thought but not advanced training.

If the position for which you are applying is technical or advanced, you will read more advanced, specialized material. If you are already familiar with the basic principles of your field, elementary textbooks would waste your time. Concentrate on advanced textbooks and technical periodicals. Think through the concepts and review difficult problems in your field.

These are all general sources. You can get more ideas on your own initiative, following these leads. For example, training manuals and publications of the government agency which employs workers in your field can be useful, particularly for technical and professional positions. A letter or visit to the government department involved may result in more specific study suggestions, and certainly will provide you with a more definite idea of the exact nature of the position you are seeking.

III. KINDS OF TESTS

Tests are used for purposes other than measuring knowledge and ability to perform specified duties. For some positions, it is equally important to test ability to make adjustments to new situations or to profit from training. In others, basic mental abilities not dependent on information are essential. Questions which test these things may not appear as pertinent to the duties of the position as those which test for knowledge and information. Yet they are often highly important parts of a fair examination. For very general questions, it is almost impossible to help you direct your study efforts. What we can do is to point out some of the more common of these general abilities needed in public service positions and describe some typical questions.

1) General information

Broad, general information has been found useful for predicting job success in some kinds of work. This is tested in a variety of ways, from vocabulary lists to questions about current events. Basic background in some field of work, such as sociology or economics, may be sampled in a group of questions. Often these are principles which have become familiar to most persons through exposure rather than through formal training. It is difficult to advise you how to study for these questions; being alert to the world around you is our best suggestion.

2) Verbal ability

An example of an ability needed in many positions is verbal or language ability. Verbal ability is, in brief, the ability to use and understand words. Vocabulary and grammar tests are typical measures of this ability. Reading comprehension or paragraph interpretation questions are common in many kinds of civil service tests. You are given a paragraph of written material and asked to find its central meaning.

3) Numerical ability

Number skills can be tested by the familiar arithmetic problem, by checking paired lists of numbers to see which are alike and which are different, or by interpreting charts and graphs. In the latter test, a graph may be printed in the test booklet which you are asked to use as the basis for answering questions.

4) Observation

A popular test for law-enforcement positions is the observation test. A picture is shown to you for several minutes, then taken away. Questions about the picture test your ability to observe both details and larger elements.

5) Following directions

In many positions in the public service, the employee must be able to carry out written instructions dependably and accurately. You may be given a chart with several columns, each column listing a variety of information. The questions require you to carry out directions involving the information given in the chart.

6) Skills and aptitudes

Performance tests effectively measure some manual skills and aptitudes. When the skill is one in which you are trained, such as typing or shorthand, you can practice. These tests are often very much like those given in business school or high school courses. For many of the other skills and aptitudes, however, no short-time preparation can be made. Skills and abilities natural to you or that you have developed throughout your lifetime are being tested.

Many of the general questions just described provide all the data needed to answer the questions and ask you to use your reasoning ability to find the answers. Your best preparation for these tests, as well as for tests of facts and ideas, is to be at your physical and mental best. You, no doubt, have your own methods of getting into an exam-taking mood and keeping "in shape." The next section lists some ideas on this subject.

IV. KINDS OF QUESTIONS

Only rarely is the "essay" question, which you answer in narrative form, used in civil service tests. Civil service tests are usually of the short-answer type. Full instructions for answering these questions will be given to you at the examination. But in case this is your first experience with short-answer questions and separate answer sheets, here is what you need to know:

1) **Multiple-choice Questions**

Most popular of the short-answer questions is the "multiple choice" or "best answer" question. It can be used, for example, to test for factual knowledge, ability to solve problems or judgment in meeting situations found at work.

A multiple-choice question is normally one of three types—
- It can begin with an incomplete statement followed by several possible endings. You are to find the one ending which *best* completes the statement, although some of the others may not be entirely wrong.
- It can also be a complete statement in the form of a question which is answered by choosing one of the statements listed.

- It can be in the form of a problem – again you select the best answer.

Here is an example of a multiple-choice question with a discussion which should give you some clues as to the method for choosing the right answer:

When an employee has a complaint about his assignment, the action which will *best* help him overcome his difficulty is to
- A. discuss his difficulty with his coworkers
- B. take the problem to the head of the organization
- C. take the problem to the person who gave him the assignment
- D. say nothing to anyone about his complaint

In answering this question, you should study each of the choices to find which is best. Consider choice "A" – Certainly an employee may discuss his complaint with fellow employees, but no change or improvement can result, and the complaint remains unresolved. Choice "B" is a poor choice since the head of the organization probably does not know what assignment you have been given, and taking your problem to him is known as "going over the head" of the supervisor. The supervisor, or person who made the assignment, is the person who can clarify it or correct any injustice. Choice "C" is, therefore, correct. To say nothing, as in choice "D," is unwise. Supervisors have and interest in knowing the problems employees are facing, and the employee is seeking a solution to his problem.

2) True/False Questions

The "true/false" or "right/wrong" form of question is sometimes used. Here a complete statement is given. Your job is to decide whether the statement is right or wrong.

SAMPLE: A roaming cell-phone call to a nearby city costs less than a non-roaming call to a distant city.

This statement is wrong, or false, since roaming calls are more expensive.

This is not a complete list of all possible question forms, although most of the others are variations of these common types. You will always get complete directions for answering questions. Be sure you understand *how* to mark your answers – ask questions until you do.

V. RECORDING YOUR ANSWERS

Computer terminals are used more and more today for many different kinds of exams.

For an examination with very few applicants, you may be told to record your answers in the test booklet itself. Separate answer sheets are much more common. If this separate answer sheet is to be scored by machine – and this is often the case – it is highly important that you mark your answers correctly in order to get credit.

An electronic scoring machine is often used in civil service offices because of the speed with which papers can be scored. Machine-scored answer sheets must be marked with a pencil, which will be given to you. This pencil has a high graphite content which responds to the electronic scoring machine. As a matter of fact, stray dots may register as answers, so do not let your pencil rest on the answer sheet while you are pondering the correct answer. Also, if your pencil lead breaks or is otherwise defective, ask for another.

Since the answer sheet will be dropped in a slot in the scoring machine, be careful not to bend the corners or get the paper crumpled.

The answer sheet normally has five vertical columns of numbers, with 30 numbers to a column. These numbers correspond to the question numbers in your test booklet. After each number, going across the page are four or five pairs of dotted lines. These short dotted lines have small letters or numbers above them. The first two pairs may also have a "T" or "F" above the letters. This indicates that the first two pairs only are to be used if the questions are of the true-false type. If the questions are multiple choice, disregard the "T" and "F" and pay attention only to the small letters or numbers.

Answer your questions in the manner of the sample that follows:

32. The largest city in the United States is
    A. Washington, D.C.
    B. New York City
    C. Chicago
    D. Detroit
    E. San Francisco

1) Choose the answer you think is best. (New York City is the largest, so "B" is correct.)
2) Find the row of dotted lines numbered the same as the question you are answering. (Find row number 32)
3) Find the pair of dotted lines corresponding to the answer. (Find the pair of lines under the mark "B.")
4) Make a solid black mark between the dotted lines.

VI. BEFORE THE TEST

Common sense will help you find procedures to follow to get ready for an examination. Too many of us, however, overlook these sensible measures. Indeed, nervousness and fatigue have been found to be the most serious reasons why applicants fail to do their best on civil service tests. Here is a list of reminders:

- Begin your preparation early – Don't wait until the last minute to go scurrying around for books and materials or to find out what the position is all about.
- Prepare continuously – An hour a night for a week is better than an all-night cram session. This has been definitely established. What is more, a night a week for a month will return better dividends than crowding your study into a shorter period of time.
- Locate the place of the exam – You have been sent a notice telling you when and where to report for the examination. If the location is in a different town or otherwise unfamiliar to you, it would be well to inquire the best route and learn something about the building.
- Relax the night before the test – Allow your mind to rest. Do not study at all that night. Plan some mild recreation or diversion; then go to bed early and get a good night's sleep.
- Get up early enough to make a leisurely trip to the place for the test – This way unforeseen events, traffic snarls, unfamiliar buildings, etc. will not upset you.
- Dress comfortably – A written test is not a fashion show. You will be known by number and not by name, so wear something comfortable.

- Leave excess paraphernalia at home – Shopping bags and odd bundles will get in your way. You need bring only the items mentioned in the official notice you received; usually everything you need is provided. Do not bring reference books to the exam. They will only confuse those last minutes and be taken away from you when in the test room.
- Arrive somewhat ahead of time – If because of transportation schedules you must get there very early, bring a newspaper or magazine to take your mind off yourself while waiting.
- Locate the examination room – When you have found the proper room, you will be directed to the seat or part of the room where you will sit. Sometimes you are given a sheet of instructions to read while you are waiting. Do not fill out any forms until you are told to do so; just read them and be prepared.
- Relax and prepare to listen to the instructions
- If you have any physical problem that may keep you from doing your best, be sure to tell the test administrator. If you are sick or in poor health, you really cannot do your best on the exam. You can come back and take the test some other time.

VII. AT THE TEST

The day of the test is here and you have the test booklet in your hand. The temptation to get going is very strong. Caution! There is more to success than knowing the right answers. You must know how to identify your papers and understand variations in the type of short-answer question used in this particular examination. Follow these suggestions for maximum results from your efforts:

1) Cooperate with the monitor

The test administrator has a duty to create a situation in which you can be as much at ease as possible. He will give instructions, tell you when to begin, check to see that you are marking your answer sheet correctly, and so on. He is not there to guard you, although he will see that your competitors do not take unfair advantage. He wants to help you do your best.

2) Listen to all instructions

Don't jump the gun! Wait until you understand all directions. In most civil service tests you get more time than you need to answer the questions. So don't be in a hurry. Read each word of instructions until you clearly understand the meaning. Study the examples, listen to all announcements and follow directions. Ask questions if you do not understand what to do.

3) Identify your papers

Civil service exams are usually identified by number only. You will be assigned a number; you must not put your name on your test papers. Be sure to copy your number correctly. Since more than one exam may be given, copy your exact examination title.

4) Plan your time

Unless you are told that a test is a "speed" or "rate of work" test, speed itself is usually not important. Time enough to answer all the questions will be provided, but this does not mean that you have all day. An overall time limit has been set. Divide the total time (in minutes) by the number of questions to determine the approximate time you have for each question.

5) Do not linger over difficult questions

If you come across a difficult question, mark it with a paper clip (useful to have along) and come back to it when you have been through the booklet. One caution if you do this – be sure to skip a number on your answer sheet as well. Check often to be sure that you have not lost your place and that you are marking in the row numbered the same as the question you are answering.

6) Read the questions

Be sure you know what the question asks! Many capable people are unsuccessful because they failed to *read* the questions correctly.

7) Answer all questions

Unless you have been instructed that a penalty will be deducted for incorrect answers, it is better to guess than to omit a question.

8) Speed tests

It is often better NOT to guess on speed tests. It has been found that on timed tests people are tempted to spend the last few seconds before time is called in marking answers at random – without even reading them – in the hope of picking up a few extra points. To discourage this practice, the instructions may warn you that your score will be "corrected" for guessing. That is, a penalty will be applied. The incorrect answers will be deducted from the correct ones, or some other penalty formula will be used.

9) Review your answers

If you finish before time is called, go back to the questions you guessed or omitted to give them further thought. Review other answers if you have time.

10) Return your test materials

If you are ready to leave before others have finished or time is called, take ALL your materials to the monitor and leave quietly. Never take any test material with you. The monitor can discover whose papers are not complete, and taking a test booklet may be grounds for disqualification.

VIII. EXAMINATION TECHNIQUES

1) Read the general instructions carefully. These are usually printed on the first page of the exam booklet. As a rule, these instructions refer to the timing of the examination; the fact that you should not start work until the signal and must stop work at a signal, etc. If there are any *special* instructions, such as a choice of questions to be answered, make sure that you note this instruction carefully.

2) When you are ready to start work on the examination, that is as soon as the signal has been given, read the instructions to each question booklet, underline any key words or phrases, such as *least, best, outline, describe* and the like. In this way you will tend to answer as requested rather than discover on reviewing your paper that you *listed without describing*, that you selected the *worst* choice rather than the *best* choice, etc.

3) If the examination is of the objective or multiple-choice type – that is, each question will also give a series of possible answers: A, B, C or D, and you are called upon to select the best answer and write the letter next to that answer on your answer paper – it is advisable to start answering each question in turn. There may be anywhere from 50 to 100 such questions in the three or four hours allotted and you can see how much time would be taken if you read through all the questions before beginning to answer any. Furthermore, if you come across a question or group of questions which you know would be difficult to answer, it would undoubtedly affect your handling of all the other questions.

4) If the examination is of the essay type and contains but a few questions, it is a moot point as to whether you should read all the questions before starting to answer any one. Of course, if you are given a choice – say five out of seven and the like – then it is essential to read all the questions so you can eliminate the two that are most difficult. If, however, you are asked to answer all the questions, there may be danger in trying to answer the easiest one first because you may find that you will spend too much time on it. The best technique is to answer the first question, then proceed to the second, etc.

5) Time your answers. Before the exam begins, write down the time it started, then add the time allowed for the examination and write down the time it must be completed, then divide the time available somewhat as follows:
    - If 3-1/2 hours are allowed, that would be 210 minutes. If you have 80 objective-type questions, that would be an average of 2-1/2 minutes per question. Allow yourself no more than 2 minutes per question, or a total of 160 minutes, which will permit about 50 minutes to review.
    - If for the time allotment of 210 minutes there are 7 essay questions to answer, that would average about 30 minutes a question. Give yourself only 25 minutes per question so that you have about 35 minutes to review.

6) The most important instruction is to *read each question* and make sure you know what is wanted. The second most important instruction is to *time yourself properly* so that you answer every question. The third most important instruction is to *answer every question*. Guess if you have to but include something for each question. Remember that you will receive no credit for a blank and will probably receive some credit if you write something in answer to an essay question. If you guess a letter – say "B" for a multiple-choice question – you may have guessed right. If you leave a blank as an answer to a multiple-choice question, the examiners may respect your feelings but it will not add a point to your score. Some exams may penalize you for wrong answers, so in such cases *only*, you may not want to guess unless you have some basis for your answer.

7) Suggestions
    a. Objective-type questions
        1. Examine the question booklet for proper sequence of pages and questions
        2. Read all instructions carefully
        3. Skip any question which seems too difficult; return to it after all other questions have been answered
        4. Apportion your time properly; do not spend too much time on any single question or group of questions

5. Note and underline key words – *all, most, fewest, least, best, worst, same, opposite*, etc.
6. Pay particular attention to negatives
7. Note unusual option, e.g., unduly long, short, complex, different or similar in content to the body of the question
8. Observe the use of "hedging" words – *probably, may, most likely*, etc.
9. Make sure that your answer is put next to the same number as the question
10. Do not second-guess unless you have good reason to believe the second answer is definitely more correct
11. Cross out original answer if you decide another answer is more accurate; do not erase until you are ready to hand your paper in
12. Answer all questions; guess unless instructed otherwise
13. Leave time for review

b. Essay questions
1. Read each question carefully
2. Determine exactly what is wanted. Underline key words or phrases.
3. Decide on outline or paragraph answer
4. Include many different points and elements unless asked to develop any one or two points or elements
5. Show impartiality by giving pros and cons unless directed to select one side only
6. Make and write down any assumptions you find necessary to answer the questions
7. Watch your English, grammar, punctuation and choice of words
8. Time your answers; don't crowd material

8) Answering the essay question

Most essay questions can be answered by framing the specific response around several key words or ideas. Here are a few such key words or ideas:

M's: manpower, materials, methods, money, management
P's: purpose, program, policy, plan, procedure, practice, problems, pitfalls, personnel, public relations

  a. Six basic steps in handling problems:
    1. Preliminary plan and background development
    2. Collect information, data and facts
    3. Analyze and interpret information, data and facts
    4. Analyze and develop solutions as well as make recommendations
    5. Prepare report and sell recommendations
    6. Install recommendations and follow up effectiveness

  b. Pitfalls to avoid
    1. *Taking things for granted* – A statement of the situation does not necessarily imply that each of the elements is necessarily true; for example, a complaint may be invalid and biased so that all that can be taken for granted is that a complaint has been registered

2. *Considering only one side of a situation* – Wherever possible, indicate several alternatives and then point out the reasons you selected the best one
3. *Failing to indicate follow up* – Whenever your answer indicates action on your part, make certain that you will take proper follow-up action to see how successful your recommendations, procedures or actions turn out to be
4. *Taking too long in answering any single question* – Remember to time your answers properly

IX. AFTER THE TEST

Scoring procedures differ in detail among civil service jurisdictions although the general principles are the same. Whether the papers are hand-scored or graded by machine we have described, they are nearly always graded by number. That is, the person who marks the paper knows only the number – never the name – of the applicant. Not until all the papers have been graded will they be matched with names. If other tests, such as training and experience or oral interview ratings have been given, scores will be combined. Different parts of the examination usually have different weights. For example, the written test might count 60 percent of the final grade, and a rating of training and experience 40 percent. In many jurisdictions, veterans will have a certain number of points added to their grades.

After the final grade has been determined, the names are placed in grade order and an eligible list is established. There are various methods for resolving ties between those who get the same final grade – probably the most common is to place first the name of the person whose application was received first. Job offers are made from the eligible list in the order the names appear on it. You will be notified of your grade and your rank as soon as all these computations have been made. This will be done as rapidly as possible.

People who are found to meet the requirements in the announcement are called "eligibles." Their names are put on a list of eligible candidates. An eligible's chances of getting a job depend on how high he stands on this list and how fast agencies are filling jobs from the list.

When a job is to be filled from a list of eligibles, the agency asks for the names of people on the list of eligibles for that job. When the civil service commission receives this request, it sends to the agency the names of the three people highest on this list. Or, if the job to be filled has specialized requirements, the office sends the agency the names of the top three persons who meet these requirements from the general list.

The appointing officer makes a choice from among the three people whose names were sent to him. If the selected person accepts the appointment, the names of the others are put back on the list to be considered for future openings.

That is the rule in hiring from all kinds of eligible lists, whether they are for typist, carpenter, chemist, or something else. For every vacancy, the appointing officer has his choice of any one of the top three eligibles on the list. This explains why the person whose name is on top of the list sometimes does not get an appointment when some of the persons lower on the list do. If the appointing officer chooses the second or third eligible, the No. 1 eligible does not get a job at once, but stays on the list until he is appointed or the list is terminated.

X. HOW TO PASS THE INTERVIEW TEST

The examination for which you applied requires an oral interview test. You have already taken the written test and you are now being called for the interview test – the final part of the formal examination.

You may think that it is not possible to prepare for an interview test and that there are no procedures to follow during an interview. Our purpose is to point out some things you can do in advance that will help you and some good rules to follow and pitfalls to avoid while you are being interviewed.

What is an interview supposed to test?

The written examination is designed to test the technical knowledge and competence of the candidate; the oral is designed to evaluate intangible qualities, not readily measured otherwise, and to establish a list showing the relative fitness of each candidate – as measured against his competitors – for the position sought. Scoring is not on the basis of "right" and "wrong," but on a sliding scale of values ranging from "not passable" to "outstanding." As a matter of fact, it is possible to achieve a relatively low score without a single "incorrect" answer because of evident weakness in the qualities being measured.

Occasionally, an examination may consist entirely of an oral test – either an individual or a group oral. In such cases, information is sought concerning the technical knowledges and abilities of the candidate, since there has been no written examination for this purpose. More commonly, however, an oral test is used to supplement a written examination.

Who conducts interviews?

The composition of oral boards varies among different jurisdictions. In nearly all, a representative of the personnel department serves as chairman. One of the members of the board may be a representative of the department in which the candidate would work. In some cases, "outside experts" are used, and, frequently, a businessman or some other representative of the general public is asked to serve. Labor and management or other special groups may be represented. The aim is to secure the services of experts in the appropriate field.

However the board is composed, it is a good idea (and not at all improper or unethical) to ascertain in advance of the interview who the members are and what groups they represent. When you are introduced to them, you will have some idea of their backgrounds and interests, and at least you will not stutter and stammer over their names.

What should be done before the interview?

While knowledge about the board members is useful and takes some of the surprise element out of the interview, there is other preparation which is more substantive. It *is* possible to prepare for an oral interview – in several ways:

1) Keep a copy of your application and review it carefully before the interview

This may be the only document before the oral board, and the starting point of the interview. Know what education and experience you have listed there, and the sequence and dates of all of it. Sometimes the board will ask you to review the highlights of your experience for them; you should not have to hem and haw doing it.

2) Study the class specification and the examination announcement

Usually, the oral board has one or both of these to guide them. The qualities, characteristics or knowledges required by the position sought are stated in these documents. They offer valuable clues as to the nature of the oral interview. For example, if the job involves supervisory responsibilities, the announcement will usually indicate that knowledge of modern supervisory methods and the qualifications of the candidate as a supervisor will be tested. If so, you can expect such questions, frequently in the form of a hypothetical situation which you are expected to solve. NEVER go into an oral without knowledge of the duties and responsibilities of the job you seek.

3) Think through each qualification required
Try to visualize the kind of questions you would ask if you were a board member. How well could you answer them? Try especially to appraise your own knowledge and background in each area, *measured against the job sought*, and identify any areas in which you are weak. Be critical and realistic – do not flatter yourself.

4) Do some general reading in areas in which you feel you may be weak
For example, if the job involves supervision and your past experience has NOT, some general reading in supervisory methods and practices, particularly in the field of human relations, might be useful. Do NOT study agency procedures or detailed manuals. The oral board will be testing your understanding and capacity, not your memory.

5) Get a good night's sleep and watch your general health and mental attitude
You will want a clear head at the interview. Take care of a cold or any other minor ailment, and of course, no hangovers.

What should be done on the day of the interview?
Now comes the day of the interview itself. Give yourself plenty of time to get there. Plan to arrive somewhat ahead of the scheduled time, particularly if your appointment is in the fore part of the day. If a previous candidate fails to appear, the board might be ready for you a bit early. By early afternoon an oral board is almost invariably behind schedule if there are many candidates, and you may have to wait. Take along a book or magazine to read, or your application to review, but leave any extraneous material in the waiting room when you go in for your interview. In any event, relax and compose yourself.

The matter of dress is important. The board is forming impressions about you – from your experience, your manners, your attitude, and your appearance. Give your personal appearance careful attention. Dress your best, but not your flashiest. Choose conservative, appropriate clothing, and be sure it is immaculate. This is a business interview, and your appearance should indicate that you regard it as such. Besides, being well groomed and properly dressed will help boost your confidence.

Sooner or later, someone will call your name and escort you into the interview room. *This is it.* From here on you are on your own. It is too late for any more preparation. But remember, you asked for this opportunity to prove your fitness, and you are here because your request was granted.

What happens when you go in?
The usual sequence of events will be as follows: The clerk (who is often the board stenographer) will introduce you to the chairman of the oral board, who will introduce you to the other members of the board. Acknowledge the introductions before you sit down. Do not be surprised if you find a microphone facing you or a stenotypist sitting by. Oral interviews are usually recorded in the event of an appeal or other review.

Usually the chairman of the board will open the interview by reviewing the highlights of your education and work experience from your application – primarily for the benefit of the other members of the board, as well as to get the material into the record. Do not interrupt or comment unless there is an error or significant misinterpretation; if that is the case, do not hesitate. But do not quibble about insignificant matters. Also, he will usually ask you some question about your education, experience or your present job – partly to get you to start talking and to establish the interviewing "rapport." He may start the actual questioning, or turn it over to one of the other members. Frequently, each member undertakes the questioning on a particular area, one in which he is perhaps most competent, so you can expect each member to participate in the examination. Because time is limited, you may also expect some rather abrupt switches in the direction the questioning takes, so do not be upset by it. Normally, a board member will not pursue a single line of questioning unless he discovers a particular strength or weakness.

After each member has participated, the chairman will usually ask whether any member has any further questions, then will ask you if you have anything you wish to add. Unless you are expecting this question, it may floor you. Worse, it may start you off on an extended, extemporaneous speech. The board is not usually seeking more information. The question is principally to offer you a last opportunity to present further qualifications or to indicate that you have nothing to add. So, if you feel that a significant qualification or characteristic has been overlooked, it is proper to point it out in a sentence or so. Do not compliment the board on the thoroughness of their examination – they have been sketchy, and you know it. If you wish, merely say, "No thank you, I have nothing further to add." This is a point where you can "talk yourself out" of a good impression or fail to present an important bit of information. Remember, *you close the interview yourself*.

The chairman will then say, "That is all, Mr. _____, thank you." Do not be startled; the interview is over, and quicker than you think. Thank him, gather your belongings and take your leave. Save your sigh of relief for the other side of the door.

How to put your best foot forward

Throughout this entire process, you may feel that the board individually and collectively is trying to pierce your defenses, seek out your hidden weaknesses and embarrass and confuse you. Actually, this is not true. They are obliged to make an appraisal of your qualifications for the job you are seeking, and they want to see you in your best light. Remember, they must interview all candidates and a non-cooperative candidate may become a failure in spite of their best efforts to bring out his qualifications. Here are 15 suggestions that will help you:

1) **Be natural – Keep your attitude confident, not cocky**

If you are not confident that you can do the job, do not expect the board to be. Do not apologize for your weaknesses, try to bring out your strong points. The board is interested in a positive, not negative, presentation. Cockiness will antagonize any board member and make him wonder if you are covering up a weakness by a false show of strength.

2) **Get comfortable, but don't lounge or sprawl**

Sit erectly but not stiffly. A careless posture may lead the board to conclude that you are careless in other things, or at least that you are not impressed by the importance of the occasion. Either conclusion is natural, even if incorrect. Do not fuss with your clothing, a pencil or an ashtray. Your hands may occasionally be useful to emphasize a point; do not let them become a point of distraction.

3) **Do not wisecrack or make small talk**

This is a serious situation, and your attitude should show that you consider it as such. Further, the time of the board is limited – they do not want to waste it, and neither should you.

4) Do not exaggerate your experience or abilities

In the first place, from information in the application or other interviews and sources, the board may know more about you than you think. Secondly, you probably will not get away with it. An experienced board is rather adept at spotting such a situation, so do not take the chance.

5) If you know a board member, do not make a point of it, yet do not hide it

Certainly you are not fooling him, and probably not the other members of the board. Do not try to take advantage of your acquaintanceship – it will probably do you little good.

6) Do not dominate the interview

Let the board do that. They will give you the clues – do not assume that you have to do all the talking. Realize that the board has a number of questions to ask you, and do not try to take up all the interview time by showing off your extensive knowledge of the answer to the first one.

7) Be attentive

You only have 20 minutes or so, and you should keep your attention at its sharpest throughout. When a member is addressing a problem or question to you, give him your undivided attention. Address your reply principally to him, but do not exclude the other board members.

8) Do not interrupt

A board member may be stating a problem for you to analyze. He will ask you a question when the time comes. Let him state the problem, and wait for the question.

9) Make sure you understand the question

Do not try to answer until you are sure what the question is. If it is not clear, restate it in your own words or ask the board member to clarify it for you. However, do not haggle about minor elements.

10) Reply promptly but not hastily

A common entry on oral board rating sheets is "candidate responded readily," or "candidate hesitated in replies." Respond as promptly and quickly as you can, but do not jump to a hasty, ill-considered answer.

11) Do not be peremptory in your answers

A brief answer is proper – but do not fire your answer back. That is a losing game from your point of view. The board member can probably ask questions much faster than you can answer them.

12) Do not try to create the answer you think the board member wants

He is interested in what kind of mind you have and how it works – not in playing games. Furthermore, he can usually spot this practice and will actually grade you down on it.

13) Do not switch sides in your reply merely to agree with a board member

Frequently, a member will take a contrary position merely to draw you out and to see if you are willing and able to defend your point of view. Do not start a debate, yet do not surrender a good position. If a position is worth taking, it is worth defending.

14) Do not be afraid to admit an error in judgment if you are shown to be wrong

The board knows that you are forced to reply without any opportunity for careful consideration. Your answer may be demonstrably wrong. If so, admit it and get on with the interview.

15) Do not dwell at length on your present job

The opening question may relate to your present assignment. Answer the question but do not go into an extended discussion. You are being examined for a *new* job, not your present one. As a matter of fact, try to phrase ALL your answers in terms of the job for which you are being examined.

Basis of Rating

Probably you will forget most of these "do's" and "don'ts" when you walk into the oral interview room. Even remembering them all will not ensure you a passing grade. Perhaps you did not have the qualifications in the first place. But remembering them will help you to put your best foot forward, without treading on the toes of the board members.

Rumor and popular opinion to the contrary notwithstanding, an oral board wants you to make the best appearance possible. They know you are under pressure – but they also want to see how you respond to it as a guide to what your reaction would be under the pressures of the job you seek. They will be influenced by the degree of poise you display, the personal traits you show and the manner in which you respond.

ABOUT THIS BOOK

This book contains tests divided into Examination Sections. Go through each test, answering every question in the margin. We have also attached a sample answer sheet at the back of the book that can be removed and used. At the end of each test look at the answer key and check your answers. On the ones you got wrong, look at the right answer choice and learn. Do not fill in the answers first. Do not memorize the questions and answers, but understand the answer and principles involved. On your test, the questions will likely be different from the samples. Questions are changed and new ones added. If you understand these past questions you should have success with any changes that arise. Tests may consist of several types of questions. We have additional books on each subject should more study be advisable or necessary for you. Finally, the more you study, the better prepared you will be. This book is intended to be the last thing you study before you walk into the examination room. Prior study of relevant texts is also recommended. NLC publishes some of these in our Fundamental Series. Knowledge and good sense are important factors in passing your exam. Good luck also helps. So now study this Passbook, absorb the material contained within and take that knowledge into the examination. Then do your best to pass that exam.

EXAMINATION SECTION

SAMPLE QUESTIONS

COMMUNICATING WITH THE PUBLIC

DIRECTIONS: Each question or incomplete statement is followed by several suggested answers or completions. Select the one that BEST answers the question or completes the statement. *PRINT THE LETTER OF THE CORRECT ANSWER IN THE SPACE AT THE RIGHT.*

1. If others are within hearing distance while you are taking a confidential phone message, the BEST way to verify that the message is correct is to
   A. read the message back to the caller
   B. ask the caller to call back later
   C. explain that you will call back
   D. ask the caller to repeat the message

   1.____

2. In order to complete a certain task, you need to ask a favor of a worker you don't know very well. The BEST way to do this would be to
   A. ask him briefly stating your reasons
   B. convince him it is for the good of the office
   C. tell him how greatly he can benefit if he does it
   D. offer to do something for him in return

   2.____

KEY (CORRECT ANSWERS)

1. The correct answer is D. If the caller repeats the message to you, the other people in the room will not hear what he is saying, and you will be able to check the facts in the message.

2. The correct answer is A. Be businesslike and to the point when you ask for a work-related favor from a fellow worker.

EXAMINATION SECTION
TEST 1

DIRECTIONS: Each question or incomplete statement is followed by several suggested answers or completions. Select the one that BEST answers the question or completes the statement. *PRINT THE LETTER OF THE CORRECT ANSWER IN THE SPACE AT THE RIGHT.*

1. Public organizations usually share each of the following customer-service problems with private organizations EXCEPT
    A. aversion to risk
    B. staff-heaviness
    C. provision of reverse incentives
    D. control-apportionment functions

    1.____

2. A service representative demonstrates interpersonal skills by
    A. identifying a customer's expectations
    B. learning how to use a new office telephone system
    C. studying a competitor's approach to service
    D. anticipating how a customer will react to certain situations

    2.____

3. Of the following, _____ is NOT generally considered to be a common reason for flaws in an organization's customer focus.
    A. commissioned employee compensation
    B. full problem-solving authority for front-line personnel
    C. inadequate hiring practices
    D. specific, case-oriented policy and procedural statements

    3.____

4. According to MOST research, approximately _____ of dissatisfied customers will actually complain or make their dissatisfaction with a product known to the organization.
    A. 5%   B. 25%   C. 50%   D. 75%

    4.____

5. Which of the following is an example of an expected benefit associated with a product or service?
    A. Before buying a car, a customer believes she will not have to take the car in for repairs every few months.
    B. A customer in a sporting goods store tells a salesperson exactly what kind of trolling motor will meet the requirements of the lakes the customer wanted to fish.
    C. A supermarket shopper buys a loaf of bread, believing that the bread will remain fresh for a few days.
    D. An airline passenger discover that the meals served on board are good.

    5.____

6. During a meeting with a service representative, a customer makes an apparently reasonable request. However, the representative knows that satisfying the customer's request will violate a rule that is part of the organization's policy. Although the representative feels that an exception to the rule should be made in this case, she is not sure whether an exception can or should be made.

    6.____

The BEST course of action for the representative would be to
A. deny the request and apologize, explaining the company policy
B. rely on good judgment and allow the request
C. try to steer the customer toward a similar but clearly permissible request
D. contact a manager or more experienced peer to handle the request

7. While organizing an effective customer service department, it would be LEAST effective to
   A. create procedures for relaying reasons for complaints to other departments
   B. set up a clear chain-of-command for handling specific customer complaints
   C. continually monitor performance of front-line personnel
   D. give front-line people full authority to resolve all customer dissatisfaction

8. Of the following, _____ is an example of *tangible* service.
   A. an interior decorator telling his/her ideas to a potential client
   B. a salesclerk giving a written cost estimate to a potential buyer
   C. an automobile salesman telling a showroom customer about a car's performance
   D. a stockbroker offering investment advice over the telephone

9. As a rule, a customer service representative who handles telephones should always answer a call within no more than _____ ring(s).
   A. 1   B. 3   C. 5   D. 8

10. In order to be as useful as possible to an organization, feedback received from customers should NOT be
    A. portrayed on a line graph or similar device
    B. used to provide a general overview
    C. focused on end-use customers
    D. available upon demand

11. Of all the customers who switch to competing organizations approximately _____ percent do so because of poor service.
    A. 25   B. 40   C. 75   D. 95

12. When customers offer information that is incorrect in their complaints, a service representative should do each of the following EXCEPT
    A. assume that the customer is making an innocent mistake
    B. look for opportunities to educate the customer
    C. calmly state a reasonable argument that will correct the customer's mistake
    D. believe the customer until he/she is able to find proof of his/her error

13. In order to insure that a customer feels comfortable in a face-to-face meeting, a service representative should
    A. avoid discussing controversial issues
    B. use personal terms such as *dear* or *friend*
    C. address the customer by his/her first name
    D. tell a few jokes

14. Customer satisfaction is MOST effectively measured in terms of
    A. cost   B. benefit   C. convenience   D. value

15. Making a sale is NOT considered good service when
    A. there are no alternatives to the subject of the customer's complaint
    B. when the original product or service is outdated
    C. an add-in feature will forestall other problems
    D. the product or service the customer has been using is the wrong product

16. When dealing with an indecisive customer, the service representative should
    A. expand available possibilities
    B. offer a way out of unsatisfying decisions
    C. ask probing questions for understanding
    D. steer the customer toward one particular decision

17. Of the following, _____ would NOT be a source of direct organizational service promises.
    A. advertising materials
    B. published organizational policies
    C. contracts
    D. the customer's past experience with the organization

18. Generally, the only kind of organization that can validly circumvent the requirements of customer service is one that
    A. cannot afford to staff an entire service department
    B. relies solely on the sale of ten or fewer items per year
    C. has little or no competition
    D. serves clients that are separated from consumers

19. When using the problem-solving approach to solve the problem of an upset customer, the service representative should FIRST
    A. express respect for the customer
    B. identify the customer's expectations
    C. outline a solution or alternatives
    D. listen to understand the problem

20. During face-to-face meetings with strangers such as service personnel, most North Americans consider a comfortable proximity to be
    A. 6 inches - 1 foot   B. 8 inches - 1½ feet
    C. 1½ - 2 feet   D. 2-4 feet

21. When answering phone calls, a service representative should ALWAYS do each 21._____
    of the following EXCEPT
    A. state his/her name
    B. give the name of the organization or department
    C. ask probing questions
    D. offer assistance

22. If a customer appears to be emotionally neutral when lodging a complaint, it 22._____
    would be MOST appropriate for a service representative to demonstrate ____
    in reaction to the complaint.
    A. urgency   B. empathy   C. nonchalance   D. surprise

23. When soliciting customer feedback, standard practice is to limit the number 23._____
    of questions asked to APPROXIMATELY
    A. 3-5   B. 5-10   C. 10-20   D. 15-40

24. A customer has purchased an item from a company and has been told that 24._____
    the item will be delivered in two weeks. However, a customer service
    representative later discovers that deliveries are running about three days
    behind schedule.
    The MOST appropriate course of action for the representative would be to
    A. call the customer immediately, apologize for the delay, and await the
       customer's response
    B. call the customer a few days before delivery is due and explain that the
       delay is the fault of the delivery company
    C. immediately sent out a *loaner* of the ordered item to the customer
    D. wait for the customer to note the delay and contact the organization

25. Most research show that _____% of what is communicated between people 25._____
    during face-to-face meetings is conveyed through words alone.
    A. 10   B. 30   C. 50   D. 80

KEY (CORRECT ANSWERS)

1.	D	11.	B
2.	D	12.	C
3.	B	13.	A
4.	A	14.	D
5.	B	15.	A
6.	D	16.	B
7.	B	17.	D
8.	B	18.	C
9.	B	19.	A
10.	B	20.	C

21.	C
22.	D
23.	B
24.	A
25.	A

TEST 2

DIRECTIONS: Each question or incomplete statement is followed by several suggested answers or completions. Select the one that BEST answers the question or completes the statement. *PRINT THE LETTER OF THE CORRECT ANSWER IN THE SPACE AT THE RIGHT.*

1. When working cooperatively to identify specific internal service targets, personnel typically encounter each of the following obstacles EXCEPT
   A. rapidly-changing work environment
   B. philosophical differences about the nature of service
   C. specialized knowledge of certain personnel exceeds that of others
   D. a chain-of-command that isolates the end user

   1.____

2. Which of the following is an example of an external customer relationship?
   A. Baggage clerks to travelers
   B. Catering staff to flight attendants
   C. Managers to ticketing agents
   D. Maintenance workers to ground crew

   2.____

3. When a service representative puts a customer's complaint in writing, results will be produced more quickly than if the representative had merely told someone.
   Which of the following is NOT generally considered to be a reason for this?
   A. The complaint can be more easily routed to parties capable of solving the problem.
   B. Management will understand the problem more clearly.
   C. The representative can more clearly see the main aspects of the complaint.
   D. The complaint and response will become a part of a public record.

   3.____

4. A customer service representative creates a client file, which contains notes about what particular clients want, need, and expect.
   Which of the following basic areas of learning is the representative exercising?
   A. Interpersonal skills   B. Product and service knowledge
   C. Customer knowledge   D. Technical skills

   4.____

5. A customer complains that a desired product, which is currently on sale, is needed in at least two weeks, but the company is out of stock and the product will not be available for another four weeks.
   Of the following, the BEST example of a service *recovery* on the part of a representative would be to
   A. apologize for the company's inability to serve the customer while expressing a wish to deal with the customer in the future
   B. attempt to steer the customer's interest toward an unrelated product
   C. offer a comparable model at the same sale price

   5.____

6. Of the following, _____ is NOT generally considered to be a function of closed questioning when dealing with a customer.
   A. understanding requests
   B. getting the customer to agree
   C. clarifying what has been said
   D. summarizing a conversation

7. When dealing with a customer who speaks with a heavy foreign accent, a service representative should NOT
   A. speak loudly
   B. speak slowly
   C. avoid humor or witticism
   D. repeat what has been said

8. If a customer service representative is aware that time will be a factor in the delivery of service to a customer, the representative should FIRST
   A. warn the customer that the organization is under time constraints
   B. suggest that the customer return another time
   C. ask the customer to suggest a service deadline
   D. tell the customer when service can reasonably be expected

9. In relation to a customer service representative's view of an organization, the customer's view of the company tends to be
   A. more negative
   B. more objective
   C. broader in scope
   D. less forgiving

10. When asked to define the factors that determine whether they will do business with an organization, most customers maintain that _____ is the MOST important.
    A. friendly employees
    B. having their needs met
    C. convenience
    D. product pricing

11. While a customer is stating her service requirements, a service representative should do each of the following EXCEPT
    A. ask questions about complex or unclear information
    B. formulate a response to the customer's remarks
    C. repeat critical information
    D. attempt to roughly outline the customer's main points

12. If a customer service representative must deal with other member of a service team in order to resolve a problem, the representative should avoid
    A. conveying every single detail of a problem to others
    B. suggesting deadlines for problem resolution
    C. offering opinions about the source of the problem
    D. explaining the specifics concerning the need for resolution

13. Of the following, the LAST step in the resolution of a service problem should be
    A. the offer of an apology for the problem
    B. asking probing questions to understand and conform the nature of the problem
    C. listening to the customer's description of the problem
    D. determining and implementing a solution to the problem

14. _____ is a poor scheduling strategy for a customer service representative. 14.____
    A. Performing the easiest tasks first
    B. Varying work routines
    C. Setting deadlines that will allow some restful work periods
    D. Doing similar jobs at the same time

15. The MOST defensible reason for the avoidance of customer satisfaction 15.____
    guarantees is
    A. buyer remorse
    B. repeated customer contact
    C. high costs
    D. ability of buyers to take advantage of guarantees

16. A customer service representative demonstrates knowledge and courtesy to 16.____
    customers and is able to convey trust, competence, and confidence.
    Of the following service factors, the representative is demonstrating
    A. assurance   B. responsiveness
    C. empathy   D. reliability

17. If a service representative is involved in sales, _____ is NOT one of the primary 17.____
    pieces of information he/she will need to supply the customer.
    A. cost of product or service   B. how the product works
    C. how to repair the product   D. available payment plans

18. A customer appears to be experiencing extreme feelings of anger and 18.____
    frustration when loading a complaint.
    The MOST appropriate reaction for a service representative to demonstrate is
    A. urgency   B. empathy   C. nonchalance   D. surprise

19. Of the following obstacles to customer service, _____ is NOT generally 19.____
    considered to be unique to public organizations.
    A. ambivalence toward clients   B. limited competition
    C. a rule-based mission   D. clients who are not really customers

20. Most customers report that the MOST frustrating aspect of waiting in line 20.____
    for service is
    A. not knowing how long they will have to wait for service
    B. rudeness on the part of the service representatives
    C. being expected to wait for service at all
    D. unfair prioritizing on the part of service representatives

21. Which of the following is an example of an *assumed benefit* associated with a 21.____
    product or service?
    A customer
    A buys a sporty sedan and finds that its tight turning ratio makes it easy to park
    B. visits a fast-food restaurant because she is in a hurry to get dinner over with

C. buys a videotape and believes it will not cause damage to her VCR
D. tells a salesman that he wants to purchase a high-status automobile

22. On an average, for every complaint received by an organization, there are actually about _____ customers who have legitimate problems.
    A. 3   B. 5   C. 15   D. 25

23. Once a customer problem is identified, each of the following should become a part of the service recovery process EXCEPT
    A. apologizing   B. an offer of compensation
    C. empathetic listening   D. sympathy

24. As a rule, customers who telephone organizations should not be put on hold for any longer than
    A. 10 seconds   B. 60 seconds
    C. 5 minutes   D. 10 minutes

25. The LEAST effective way to make customers feel as if they are a part of a service team would be to ask them for
    A. information about similar products/services they have used
    B. opinions about how to solve problems
    C. personally contact the department that can best help them
    D. opinions about particular products and services

KEY (CORRECT ANSWERS)

1.	B	11.	B
2.	A	12.	C
3.	D	13.	A
4.	C	14.	A
5.	D	15.	B
6.	A	16.	A
7.	A	17.	C
8.	C	18.	B
9.	C	19.	B
10.	B	20.	A

21. C
22. D
23. D
24. B
25. C

EXAMINATION SECTION
TEST 1

DIRECTIONS: Each question or incomplete statement is followed by several suggested answers or completions. Select the one that BEST answers the question or completes the statement. *PRINT THE LETTER OF THE CORRECT ANSWER IN THE SPACE AT THE RIGHT.*

1. When conducting a needs assessment for the purpose of education planning, an agency's FIRST step is to identify or provide
    A. a profile of population characteristics
    B. barriers to participation
    C. existing resources
    D. profiles of competing resources

    1.____

2. Research has demonstrated that of the following, the MOST effective medium for communicating with external publics is(are)
    A. video news releases
    B. television
    C. radio
    D. newspapers

    2.____

3. Basic ideas behind the effort to influence the attitudes and behaviors of a constituency include each of the following EXCEPT the idea that
    A. words, rather than actions or events, are most likely to motivate
    B. demands for action are a usual response
    C. self-interest usually figures heavily into public involvement
    D. the reliability of change programs is difficult to assess

    3.____

4. An agency representative is trying to craft a pithy message to constituents in order to encourage the use of agency program resources.
   Choosing an audience for such messages is easiest when the message
    A. is project- or behavior-based
    B. is combined with other messages
    C. is abstract
    D. has a broad appeal

    4.____

5. Of the following factors, the MOST important to the success of an agency's external education or communication programs is the
    A. amount of resources used to implement them
    B. public's prior experiences with the agency
    C. real value of the program to the public
    D. commitment of the internal audience

    5.____

6. A representative for a state agency is being interviewed by a reporter from a local news network. The representative is being asked to defend a program that is extremely unpopular in certain parts of the municipality.
   When a constituency is known to be opposed to a position, the MOST useful communication strategy is to present

    6.____

A. only the arguments that are consistent with constituents' views
B. only the agency's side of the issue
C. both sides of the argument as clearly as possible
D. both sides of the argument, omitting key information about the opposing position

7. The MOST significant barriers to effective agency community relations include
   I. widespread distrust of communication strategies
   II. the media's "watchdog" stance
   III. public apathy
   IV. statutory opposition

   The CORRECT answer is:
   A. I only   B. I and II   C. II and III   D. III and IV

8. In conducting an education program, many agencies use workshops and seminars in a classroom setting.
   Advantages of classroom-style teaching over other means of educating the public include each of the following, EXCEPT
   A. enabling an instructor to verify learning through testing and interaction with the target audience
   B. enabling hands-on practice and other participatory learning techniques
   C. ability to reach an unlimited number of participants in a given length of time
   D. ability to convey the latest, most up-to-date information

9. The _____ model of community relations is characterized by an attempt to persuade the public to adopt the agency's point of view.
   A. two-way symmetric   B. two-way asymmetric
   C. public information   D. press agency/publicity

10. Important elements of an internal situation analysis include the
    I. list of agency opponents   II. communication audit
    III. updated organizational almanac   IV. stakeholder analysis

    The CORRECT answer is:
    A. I and II   B. I, II, and III   C. II and III   D. I, II, III and IV

11. Government agency information efforts typically involve each of the following objectives, EXCEPT to
    A. implement changes in the policies of government agencies to align with public opinion
    B. communicate the work of agencies
    C. explain agency techniques in a way that invites input from citizens
    D. provide citizen feedback to government administrators

12. Factors that are likely to influence the effectiveness of an educational campaign include the
    I. level of homogeneity among intended participants
    II. number and types of media used
    III. receptivity of the intended participants
    IV. level of specificity in the message or behavior to be taught

    The CORRECT answer is:
    A. I and II   B. I, II, and III   C. II and III   D. I, II, III, and IV

13. An agency representative is writing instructional objectives that will later help to measure the effectiveness of an educational program.
    Which of the following verbs, included in an objective, would be MOST helpful for the purpose of measuring effectiveness?
    A. Know   B. Identify   C. Learn   D. Comprehend

14. A state education agency wants to encourage participation in a program that has just received a boost through new federal legislation. The program is intended to include participants from a wide variety of socioeconomic and other demographic characteristics. The agency wants to launch a broad-based program that will inform virtually every interested party in the state about the program's new circumstances.
    In attempting to deliver this message to such a wide-ranging constituency, the agency's BEST practice would be to
    A. broadcast the same message through as many different media channels as possible
    B. focus on one discrete segment of the public at a time
    C. craft a message whose appeal is as broad as the public itself
    D. let the program's achievements speak for themselves and rely on word-of-mouth

15. Advantages associated with using the World Wide Web as an educational tool include
    I. an appeal to younger generations of the public
    II. visually-oriented, interactive learning
    III. learning that is not confined by space, time, or institutional association
    IV. a variety of methods for verifying use and learning

    The CORRECT answer is:
    A. I only   B. I and II   C. I, II, and III   D. I, II, II, and IV

16. In agencies involved in health care, community relations is a critical function because it
    A. serves as an intermediary between the agency and consumers
    B. generates a clear mission statement for agency goals and priorities
    C. ensures patient privacy while satisfying the media's right to information
    D. helps marketing professionals determine the wants and needs of agency constituents

17. After an extensive campaign to promote its newest program to constituents, an agency learns that most of the audience did not understand the intended message.
MOST likely, the agency has
    A. chosen words that were intended to inform, rather than persuade
    B. not accurately interpreted what the audience really needed to know
    C. overestimated the ability of the audience to receive and process the message
    D. compensated for noise that may have interrupted the message

18. The necessary elements that lead to conviction and motivation in the minds of participants in an educational or information program include each of the following, EXCEPT the _____ of the message.
    A. acceptability   B. intensity
    C. single-channel appeal   D. pervasiveness

19. Printed materials are often at the core of educational programs provided by public agencies.
The PRIMARY disadvantage associated with print is that it
    A. does not enable comprehensive treatment of a topic
    B. is generally unreliable in term of assessing results
    C. is often the most expensive medium available
    D. is constrained by time

20. Traditional thinking on public opinion holds that there is about _____ percent of the public who are pivotal to shifting the balance and momentum of opinion—they are concerned about an issue, but not fanatical, and interested enough to pay attention to a reasoned discussion.
    A. 2   B. 10   C. 33   D. 51

21. One of the most useful guidelines for influencing attitude change among people is to
    A. invite the target audience to come to you, rather than approaching them
    B. use moral appeals as the primary approach
    C. use concrete images to enable people to see the results of behaviors or indifference
    D. offer tangible rewards to people for changes in behavior

22. An agency is attempting to evaluate the effectiveness of its educational program. For this purpose, it wants to observe several focus groups discussing the same program.
Which of the following would NOT be a guideline for the use of focus groups?
    A. Focus groups should only include those who have participated in the program.
    B. Be sure to accurately record the discussion.
    C. The same questions should be asked at each focus group meeting.
    D. It is often helpful to have a neutral, non-agency employee facilitate discussions.

23. Research consistently shows that _____ is the determinant most likely to make a newspaper editor run a news release.
   A. novelty   B. prominence   C. proximity   D. conflict

24. Which of the following is NOT one of the major variables to take into account when considering a population-needs assessment?
   A. State of program development   B. Resources available
   C. Demographics   D. Community attitudes

25. The FIRST step in any communications audit is to
   A. develop a research instrument
   B. determine how the organization currently communicates
   C. hire a contractor
   D. determine which audience to assess

KEY (CORRECT ANSWERS)

1. A
2. D
3. A
4. A
5. D

6. C
7. D
8. C
9. B
10. C

11. A
12. D
13. B
14. B
15. C

16. A
17. B
18. C
19. B
20. B

21. C
22. A
23. C
24. C
25. D

TEST 2

DIRECTIONS: Each question or incomplete statement is followed by several suggested answers or completions. Select the one that BEST answers the question or completes the statement. *PRINT THE LETTER OF THE CORRECT ANSWER IN THE SPACE AT THE RIGHT.*

1. A public relations practitioner at an agency has just composed a press release highlighting a program's recent accomplishments and success stories.
   In pitching such releases to print outlets, the practitioner should
   I. e-mail, mail, or send them by messenger
   II. address them to "editor" or "news director"
   III. have an assistant call all media contacts by telephone
   IV. ask reporters or editors how they prefer to receive them

   The CORRECT answer is:
   A. I and II   B. I and IV   C. II, III, and IV   D. III only

   1.____

2. The "output goals" of an educational program are MOST likely to include
   A. specified ratings of services by participants on a standardized scale
   B. observable effects on a given community or clientele
   C. the number of instructional hours provided
   D. the number of participants served

   2.____

3. An agency wants to evaluate satisfaction levels among program participants, and mails out questionnaires to everyone who has been enrolled in the last year.
   The PRIMARY problem associated with this method of evaluative research is that it
   A. poses a significant inconvenience for respondents
   B. is inordinately expensive
   C. does not allow for follow-up or clarification questions
   D. usually involves a low response rate

   3.____

4. A communications audit is an important tool for measuring
   A. the depth of penetration of a particular message or program
   B. the cost of the organization's information campaigns
   C. how key audiences perceive an organization
   D. the commitment of internal stakeholders

   4.____

5. The "ABCs" of written learning objectives include each of the following, EXCEPT
   A. Audience   B. Behavior   C. Conditions   D. Delineation

   5.____

6. When attempting to change the behaviors of constituents, it is important to keep in mind that
   I. most people are skeptical of communications that try to get them to change their behaviors
   II. in most cases, a person selects the media to which he exposes himself
   III. people tend to react defensively to messages or programs that rely on fear as a motivating factor
   IV. programs should aim for the broadest appeal possible in order to include as many participants as possible

   The CORRECT answer is:
   A. I and II   B. I, II and III   C. II and III   D. I, II, III, and IV

6._____

7. The "laws" of public opinion include the idea that it is
   A. useful for anticipating emergencies
   B. not sensitive to important events
   C. basically determined by self-interest
   D. sustainable through persistent appeals

7._____

8. Which of the following types of evaluations is used to measure public attitudes before and after an information/educational program?
   A. Retrieval study   B. Copy test
   C. Quota sampling   D. Benchmark study

8._____

9. The PRIMARY source for internal communications is(are) usually
   A. flow charts   B. meetings
   C. voice mail   D. printed publications

9._____

10. An agency representative is putting together informational materials—brochures and a newsletter—outlining changes in one of the state's biggest benefits programs.
    In assembling print materials as a medium for delivering information to the public, the representative should keep in mind each of the following trends:
    I. For various reasons, the reading capabilities of the public are in general decline
    II. Without tables and graphs to help illustrate the changes, it is unlikely that the message will be delivered effectively
    III. Professionals and career-oriented people are highly receptive to information written in the form of a journal article or empirical study
    IV. People tend to be put off by print materials that use itemized and bulleted (●) lists

    The CORRECT answer is:
    A. I and II   B. I, II and III   C. II and III   D. I, II, III, and IV

10._____

11. Which of the following steps in a problem-oriented information campaign would typically be implemented FIRST?
    A. Deciding on tactics
    B. Determining a communications strategy
    C. Evaluating the problem's impact
    D. Developing an organizational strategy

12. A common pitfall in conducting an educational program is to
    A. aim it at the wrong target audience
    B. overfund it
    C. leave it in the hands of people who are in the business of education, rather than those with expertise in the business of the organization
    D. ignore the possibility that some other organization is meeting the same educational need for the target audience

13. The key factors that affect the credibility of an agency's educational program include
    A. organization
    B. scope
    C. sophistication
    D. penetration

14. Research on public opinion consistently demonstrates that it is
    A. easy to move people toward a strong opinion on anything, as long as they are approached directly through their emotions
    B. easier to move people away from an opinion they currently hold than to have them form an opinion about something they have not previously cared about
    C. easy to move people toward a strong opinion on anything, as long as the message appeals to their reason and intellect
    D. difficult to move people toward a strong opinion on anything, no matter what the approach

15. In conducting an education program, many agencies use meetings and conferences to educate an audience about the organization and its programs. Advantages associated with this approach include
    I. a captive audience that is known to be interested in the topic
    II. ample opportunities for verifying learning
    III. cost-efficient meeting space
    IV. the ability to provide information on a wider variety of subjects

    The CORRECT answer is:
    A. I and II   B. I, III and IV   C. II and III   D. I, II, III and IV

16. An agency is attempting to evaluate the effectiveness of its educational programs. For this purpose, it wants to observe several focus groups discussing particular programs.
    For this purpose, a focus group should never number more than _____ participants.
    A. 5   B. 10   C. 15   D. 20

17. A _____ speech is written so that several agency members can deliver it to different audiences with only minor variations.
    A. basic   B. printed   C. quota   D. pattern

18. Which of the following statements about public opinion is generally considered to be FALSE?
    A. Opinion is primarily reactive rather than proactive.
    B. People have more opinions about goals than about the means by which to achieve them.
    C. Facts tend to shift opinion in the accepted direction when opinion is not solidly structured.
    D. Public opinion is based more on information than desire.

19. An agency is trying to promote its educational program.
    As a general rule, the agency should NOT assume that
    A. people will only participate if they perceive an individual benefit
    B. promotions need to be aimed at small, discrete groups
    C. if the program is good, the audience will find out about it
    D. a variety of methods, including advertising, special events, and direct mail, should be considered

20. In planning a successful educational program, probably the first and most important question for an agency to ask is:
    A. What will be the content of the program?
    B. Who will be served by the program?
    C. When is the best time to schedule the program?
    D. Why is the program necessary?

21. Media kits are LEAST likely to contain
    A. fact sheets   B. memoranda
    C. photographs with captions   D. news releases

22. The use of pamphlets and booklets as media for communication with the public often involves the disadvantage that
    A. the messages contained within them are frequently nonspecific
    B. it is difficult to measure their effectiveness in delivering the message
    C. there are few opportunities for people to refer to them
    D. color reproduction is poor

23. The MOST important prerequisite of a good educational program is an
    A. abundance of resources to implement it
    B. individual staff unit formed for the purpose of program delivery
    C. accurate needs assessment
    D. uneducated constituency

24. After an education program has been delivered, an agency conducts a program evaluation to determine whether its objectives have been met.
General rules about how to conduct such an education program valuation include each of the following, EXCEPT that it
   A. must be done immediately after the program has been implemented
   B. should be simple and easy to use
   C. should be designed so that tabulation of responses can take place quickly and inexpensively
   D. should solicit mostly subjective, open-ended responses if the audience was large

25. Using electronic media such as television as means of educating the public is typically recommended ONLY for agencies that
   I. have a fairly simple message to begin with
   II. want to reach the masses, rather than a targeted audience
   III. have substantial financial resources
   IV. accept that they will not be able to measure the results of the campaign with much precision

   The CORRECT answer is:
   A. I and II   B. I, II and III   C. II and IV   D. I, II, III and IV

KEY (CORRECT ANSWERS)

1.	B		11.	C
2.	C		12.	D
3.	D		13.	A
4.	C		14.	D
5.	D		15.	B
6.	B		16.	B
7.	C		17.	D
8.	D		18.	D
9.	D		19.	C
10.	A		20.	D

21.	B
22.	B
23.	C
24.	D
25.	D

EXAMINATION SECTION
TEST 1

DIRECTIONS: Each question or incomplete statement is followed by several suggested answers or completions. Select the one that BEST answers the question or completes the statement. *PRINT THE LETTER OF THE CORRECT ANSWER IN THE SPACE AT THE RIGHT.*

1. Which of the following is LEAST likely to be included in an accession record? 1.____

   A. Source
   B. Budgetary fund
   C. Accession number
   D. Price paid

2. A user is seeking popular information about recent political events in the United States. Which of the following indexes should be used? 2.____

   A. *Social Science Index*
   B. *MLA International Bibliography*
   C. *Lexis-Nexis Academic*
   D. *EBSCO Military and Government*

3. Which of the following is NOT a Boolean search term? 3.____

   A. AND
   B. NOT
   C. IF
   D. OR

4. A field in a MARC record is tagged "910." The field contains data 4.____

   A. about the edition
   B. of local interest
   C. for control purposes
   D. about the title

5. In _____ indexing, an algorithm is applied by a computer to the title and/or text of a work to identify and extract words and phrases representing subjects. 5.____

   A. assignment
   B. derivative
   C. automatic
   D. string

6. Most books and periodical articles receive more than one subject heading because 6.____
   I. the more headings a book or article receives, the more chances a searcher has to locate it
   II. most books and articles cover more than one subject
   III. this is a task for which most libraries are notoriously over staffed
   IV. they are classified by more than one person, on more than one occasion

   A. I only   B. I and II   C. II only   D. II, III and IV

7. The National Media Library defines two types of storage environments in digital libraries: access storage and archive storage. Which of the following statements is TRUE?

   A. Access storage has a humidity requirement significantly lower than archival storage.
   B. Archival storage involves a significantly lower temperature set point than access storage.
   C. Archival storage ensures a much longer media life expectancy.
   D. The conditions of access storage don't always allow immediate access or playback.

8. After deciding to offer users online access to an electronic journals collection through the library's online catalog, a library must decide whether to use the "single-record" or "separate-record" approach to offering access to print and electronic versions. Which of the following statements is FALSE?

   A. The separate-record approach is preferred when the online version has significant additional content not present in the original.
   B. The separate-record approach generally offers less expensive, faster access.
   C. The single-record approach is considered MOST valid when the online version contains sufficient full text to be a good substitute, and contains no significant additional content.
   D. The single-record approach is commonly applied when the online version lacks full test or has only full text from the original, and is therefore not considered to be an adequate substitute.

9. In the Library of Congress classification, numbers that begin with L are typically associated with

   A. music
   B. physical science
   C. law
   D. education

10. The trend toward outsourcing library services has proved beneficial for the bottom line of many libraries. In general, however, the outsourcing of _____ has proven to be the most controversial for libraries.

    A. conservation and preservation
    B. acquisitions plans
    C. cataloging and selection
    D. physical processing

11. In _____ level cataloging, an encoding level developed for use in the Program for Cooperative Cataloging (PCC), fields of fixed length are fully coded, but a list of exceptions applies to certain fields of variable length.

    A. full   B. core
    C. minimal   D. collection

12. In a markup language such as HTML, the basic units of information are known as 12._____

    A. entities
    B. items
    C. elements
    D. fields

13. Speed of transmission over a network is sometimes negatively affected by applications such as "bandwidth hogs." Which of the following type of file is LEAST likely to compromise the transmission speed of a network? 13._____

    A. RealAudio
    B. MP3
    C. PDF
    D. Windows Media

14. Potential library uses for computer workstations include 14._____
    I. Internet access tool
    II. management/administrative tool
    III. interlibrary loan management
    IV. collection control

    A. I and II
    B. I, II and III
    C. II and III
    D. I, II, III and IV

15. A search of a database containing 100 records relevant to a topic retrieves 75 records, 25 of which are relevant to the topic. The search is said to have _____ percent precision, or relevance ratio. 15._____

    A. 25
    B. 33
    C. 50
    D. 75

16. A typical use of JavaScript is to 16._____

    A. developing the user interface at the server side
    B. execute instructions written in a high-level language
    C. store Java application for use on a single workstation, for use in any online activity initiated by the user
    D. check data that a user provides as input as soon as it has been typed, rather than transmit it back to the server for validation

17. The TIFF and JPEG standards for representing digital images, while in many ways superior to the GIF format, present challenges in association with 17._____

    A. accessibility
    B. platform independence
    C. resolution
    D. preservation

18. In library cataloging, _____ are used to indicate interpolation, and to enclose the general material designation that follows the title in a bibliographic record that represents a nonbook item.

    A. parentheses
    B. square brackets
    C. italics
    D. bold letters

19. To locate appropriate subject headings for a preliminary search, patrons should use

    A. EBSCO Information Services
    B. the ERIC *Thesaurus*
    C. an abstract journal
    D. *Library of Congress Subject Headings*

20. Which of the following is an advantage associated with the "film-first" approach to preservation-in which microfilm records are later scanned to produce digital records?

    A. Excellent quality maintenance over generations of analog reproduction
    B. High-resolution photographic process
    C. Opportunity for image enhancement during image capture
    D. High dynamic range for complex images

21. The weeding policies of most public libraries are based on the criterion of

    A. usage
    B. content
    C. subject area
    D. date of publication

22. When making use of interlibrary loan services, a user must typically have done each of the following, EXCEPT

    A. provided bibliographic information
    B. requested a specific title
    C. seen the material to be borrowed
    D. provided references to citations of the materials

23. Which of the following is an electronic bibliographic utility?

    A. *GOBI*   B. *ProQuest*
    C. *OCLC*   D. *ODLIS*

24. The criteria for the modes of access a library is willing to accept and support is one of the most important parts of an electronic journal collection policy. The library will typically need to develop a stance on _____ as part of these criteria.

    I. simultaneous use
    II. user definition
    III. subject parameters
    IV. comprehensiveness of full text

    A. I and II
    B. I, II and IV
    C. II, III and IV
    D. I, II, III and IV

25. The Children's Internet Protection Act of 2000
    I. pegged the government-mandated discount on Internet access to compliance with certain filtering practices
    II. provided funds for libraries to implement filtering
    III. established local control over Internet access
    IV. was ruled unconstitutional by the Supreme Court.

    A. I and II
    B. II only
    C. II, III and IV
    D. I, II, III and IV

KEY (CORRECT ANSWERS)

1. B	6. B	11. B	16. D	21. A
2. C	7. B	12. A	17. D	22. C
3. C	8. B	13. C	18. B	23. C
4. B	9. D	14. D	19. D	24. A
5. C	10. C	15. B	20. B	25. A

TEST 2

DIRECTIONS: Each question or incomplete statement is followed by several suggested answers or completions. Select the one that BEST answers the question or completes the statement. *PRINT THE LETTER OF THE CORRECT ANSWER IN THE SPACE AT THE RIGHT.*

1. In cataloging, the purpose of a scope note is to

    A. indicate that a term is used as a subheading under one or more categories of headings
    B. direct a cataloger to classify works in multiple locations
    C. instruct a Dewey Decimal cataloger to append to a given base number one or more numbers found elsewhere in the classification, in order to build a class number
    D. indicate the intended use or meaning of a term in an indexing language, and any special rules for assigning it in indexing.

2. The imprint of a book includes the

    A. printing history
    B. editor's name
    C. edition of the book
    D. publisher's name

3. Which of the following is NOT an electronic periodical reference tool?

    A. *InfoTrac*
    B. *ProQuest*
    C. *EBSCOhost*
    D. *GOBI*

4. The first part of a full URL designates a

    A. protocol
    B. domain name
    C. file
    D. port

5. The FIRST step in writing a library's technology plan is typically to

    A. investigate existing options and opportunities
    B. conduct a needs assessment
    C. create a budget
    D. inventory the current technology

6. In electronic journal publishing, vendor gateways may offer
    I. a single interface for browsing journals from different publishers
    II. alerting services
    III. an electronic archive for selected titles
    IV. management reports for collection development and budgeting

    A. I only   B. I and II
    C. I, III and IV   D. I, II, III and IV

7. Which of the following electronic discussion groups focuses on school librarians and school library issues?

    A. SYSLIB-L
    B. Web4Lib
    C. LIBSOFT
    D. LM_NET

8. Each of the following is a listserv designed to announce the online availability of new journals, EXCEPT

    A. Highwire Press
    B. Fulltext Sources Online
    C. ECO
    D. Catchword

9. The _____ fields in the MARC system contain control information, numbers, and codes.

    A. 0XX
    B. 1XX
    C. 5XX
    D. 8XX

10. In Internet user, instead of being taken to a desired Web page, instead is taken to a page that says *Error Message 400*. What has happened?

    A. A password has been set up on the server for access.
    B. The file has been moved or deleted, or the URL in incorrect.
    C. Special permission is needed to access the site.
    D. The syntax used in the URL is incorrect.

11. What is the term for an electronic database that is used to translate between different representations of geospatial references-such as place names and geographic coordinates?

    A. Atlas
    B. Gazetteer
    C. GPS
    D. Mapquest

12. In the library literature, materials designated with the collecting level "1" in relation to a given subject are considered

    A. "out of scope"
    B. useful as a comprehensive resource
    C. useful as a source of minimal information
    D. a potential resource for study or instructional support

13. ANSI/NISO standards for abstracting specify that each of the following should be used in writing an abstract, EXCEPT

    A. definitions
    B. the past tense
    C. background of a study
    D. articles and conjunctions

14. In a searchable online database, a user types the following term: *children and violence and ((television or media) not cartoon)*. The use of parentheses is an example of the technique known as

    A. expansion
    B. truncation
    C. stringing
    D. nesting

15. Each of the following is an advantage associated with searching for information online, EXCEPT that

    A. users can combine search terms
    B. the information is usually more accurate than in print sources
    C. the information is updated more frequently
    D. online searches are usually faster

16. The principal advantage associated with the use of hard disk drives for digital information storage is that they

    A. are formatted into tracks and sectors
    B. don't use the binder/substrate structure that can limit physical longevity
    C. use more than one laser
    D. offer rapid, direct access to information

17. _____ rights are granted for the reprinting of a work in its entirety in an anthology

    A. Volume
    B. Serial
    C. First
    D. Subsidiary

18. Subject encyclopedias are well-suited to undergraduate research because

    A. they have been endorsed by experts in the field
    B. their articles are written by laypersons
    C. they offer broad knowledge that serves as a solid initial encounter with knowledge
    D. they often provide bibliographies to additional sources

19. What is the term for a text file on a computer that stores personal preferences used by a specific server?

    A. Cookie
    B. Applet
    C. Bot
    D. Proxy

20. In book sales, the typical library discount is _____ percent.

    A. 1-5
    B. 5-10
    C. 15-25
    D. 30-45

21. An article is cited from a well-known reference book using the MLA format. Which of the following, even if known, is LEAST likely to be included in the citation?

    A. Publisher
    B. Author
    C. Date of publication
    D. Title of article

22. In _____ indexing, a set of indexing terms is assigned to a document by a human indexer, and then the terms are manipulated by computer to create an index in which each term is listed in correct alphabetical sequence, providing access to the document under each of the terms.

    A. string
    B. automatic
    C. pre-coordinate
    D. derivative

23. Which of the following MARC tags is NOT frequently used in cataloging books?

    A. 010
    B. 246
    C. 480
    D. 651

24. A measure of the effectiveness of information retrieval, computed as the ratio of nonrelevant entries or items retrieved in response to a query to the total number of nonrelevant items indexed in the database, is

    A. fallout
    B. recall
    C. false drops
    D. precision

25. The Library of Congress subject heading "Forests and forestry" is an example of a(n) _____ indexing term.

    A. aggregate
    B. hierarchical
    C. unitary
    D. associative

KEY (CORRECT ANSWERS)

1. D	6. D	11. B	16. D	21. A
2. D	7. D	12. C	17. A	22. A
3. D	8. B	13. C	18. D	23. C
4. A	9. A	14. D	19. A	24. A
5. D	10. D	15. B	20. B	25. C

EXAMINATION SECTION
TEST 1

DIRECTIONS: Each question or incomplete statement is followed by several suggested answers or completions. Select the one that BEST answers the question or completes the statement. *PRINT THE LETTER OF THE CORRECT ANSWER IN THE SPACE AT THE RIGHT.*

1. Electronic library catalogs and periodical indexes differ from Web search engines in each of the following ways, EXCEPT that 1.____

    A. they put cataloged and indexed information through an editorial and publishing process
    B. they contain information that is cataloged and indexed by computers
    C. they can be searched by subject headings that are assigned by the indexer
    D. they include only information that has been selected by an indexer

2. The contents of a typical reference book are about _____ than the book's copyright date 2.____

    A. a year newer
    B. a year older
    C. two years older
    D. three years older

3. An acceptable use policy 3.____

    A. identifies access-blocking rules for filtering software
    B. explains First Amendment protections of freedom of speech in the library
    C. defines a curriculum for teaching users ethical and responsible computer use
    D. states the rules that govern computer, network and/or Internet use and the consequences of violations

4. Which of the following would NOT be a reason for a library staff's decision to develop an expert system? 4.____

    A. There is high staff turnover
    B. The problem is repetitive and expensive.
    C. Human experts are widely available.
    D. The problem is complex.

5. Elements of a library security plan, organized by a library security officer, typically include 5.____
    I. acceptable use policy/policies for online resources
    II. a survey of the library's collections
    III. standard operating procedures for dealing with theft
    IV. a review of the physical layout

    A. I and II
    B. I and III
    C. II, III and IV
    D. I, II, III and IV

6. Some library systems contain auxiliary systems programs that are initiated at startup and executed in the background to perform a task when needed-for example, checking incoming e-mail messages for addresses that cannot be found. These programs are known as

   A. bots
   B. crawlers
   C. macros
   D. daemons

7. The programming interface that enables a Web browser to be an interface to information services other than Web sites is a(n)

   A. DOI
   B. CGI
   C. OPAC
   D. GUI

8. HTML is most appropriate for delivering

   A. business-to-business e-commerce
   B. documents that originated from paper
   C. dynamic data
   D. static information

9. The semantic relationship between the words "bibliography" and "heading" is

   A. generic
   B. passive
   C. associative
   D. partitive

10. The Online Computer Library Center (OCLC) has established a set of input standards for entering bibliographic data into its online union catalog. Data generated by the cataloging system that cannot be altered by the cataloger is denoted

    A. R
    B. SS
    C. X
    D. O

11. What is the term for the form of the book as it is used today?

    A. Incipit
    B. Folio
    C. Index
    D. Codex

12. In indexing, a parenthetical qualifier is likely to be used for each of the following, EXCEPT to

    A. distinguish homographs
    B. give the context of an obscure word or phrase

C. indicate the intended use or meaning of the term in the indexing language
D. specify the academic discipline in which a subject is studied

13. The common measurement of the internal speed of a computer's processor is

    A. megahertz (MHz)
    B. bits per second (bps)
    C. kilobytes per second (Kbps)
    D. gigabytes (GB)

14. In _____ classification, each subject is developed to the point of indivisibility and a notation assigned for every subdivision

    A. hierarchical
    B. enumerative
    C. synthetic
    D. dichotomous

15. In Walford's *Guide to Reference Material*, religion is included in the same volume as

    A. literature
    B. social sciences
    C. humanities
    D. generalia

16. A group of librarians is meeting to determine the selection of electronic journals for a library's collection. One of the MOST likely disadvantages of including the existing electronic resources coordinator in this group is that she may not

    A. have the expertise for many of the subjects
    B. understand the issues or technology involved
    C. have the motivation or commitment
    D. be in a position to develop access interfaces

17. Which of the following is NOT a general review publication?

    A. *Quill & Quire*
    B. *CHOICE*
    C. *Lambda Book Report*
    D. *Booklist*

18. In networking, a cable is plugged into the _____ of each workstation on the network.

    A. NIC
    B. GUI
    C. LAN
    D. twisted pair

19. The PDF format is MOST typically used to transmit and store

    A. static data
    B. business-to-business e-commerce documents
    C. visually rich content
    D. database output

20. The turnover rate for media items in a library is usually measured in

    A. hours
    B. days
    C. weeks
    D. months

21. Which of the following is considered the basis of a "collection-centered" method for evaluating a library collection?

    A. Percent of relative use (PRU)
    B. In-house use studies
    C. Comparison to recommended lists
    D. Interlibrary loan statistics

22. In a MARC record for an electronic journal database, the _____ field contains the URL to the database, but not to any specific journal title.

    A. 538
    B. 710
    C. 856
    D. 949

23. Which of the following is a device used to scan and audibly read the information printed on a written page?

    A. Screen-reading software
    B. OCR software
    C. Kurzweil Reader
    D. TTY

24. A regional public library has ordered a packaged electronic journals database. The vendor asks for the "class" of the library's network. The systems librarian doesn't quite know how to answer this. She knows that the network accommodates 256 IP addresses. This network would be considered a class

    A. A
    B. B
    C. C
    D. D

25. From the library's point of view, a license agreement with an electronic journal publisher or packager should
    I. indemnify the publisher against third-party claims
    II. permit access to users who are off-site
    III. provide for archiving of content if publication or service ceases
    IV. define hardware, browser, and networking requirements

    A. I and II
    B. I and IV
    C. II, III and IV
    D. I, II, III and IV

KEY (CORRECT ANSWERS)

1. B
2. B
3. D
4. C
5. C

6. D
7. B
8. D
9. D
10. B

11. D
12. C
13. A
14. B
15. B

16. A
17. C
18. A
19. C
20. B

21. C
22. C
23. C
24. C
25. C

TEST 2

DIRECTIONS: Each question or incomplete statement is followed by several suggested answers or completions. Select the one that BEST answers the question or completes the statement. *PRINT THE LETTER OF THE CORRECT ANSWER IN THE SPACE AT THE RIGHT.*

1. The Digital Millenium Copyright Act of 1998 provides for each of the following, EXCEPT a(n) 1.___

    A. prohibition against circumventing technological measures used to protect copyrighted works
    B. limitation of liability for online service providers
    C. prohibition against altering information imbedded in digital works by copyright owners
    D. extension of the term of copyright to the author's lifetime plus 70 years

2. In the URL *http://www.sparkslib.org:80/index.html*, the *80* is a reference to a 2.___

    A. parameter
    B. file
    C. port
    D. protocol

3. Which of the following assistive technologies offers patrons who have difficulty hearing a means of communicating with library staff members? 3.___

    A. Touchpad or trackball controller
    B. TTY
    C. On-screen keyboard
    D. Screen-reading software

4. A user wants access to SEC filings of public companies on the Internet, including prospectuses, annual reports, 10K reports, and 10Q reports. The user should be directed to 4.___

    A. www.sec.gov
    B. the Thomas Register
    C. Lexis/Nexis
    D. EDGAR

5. Which of the following is a term for a software program that searches intelligently for information on the World Wide Web? 5.___

    A. Daemon
    B. Pathfinder
    C. Crawler
    D. Sorter

6. In a MARC record for an electronic journal that is separately cataloged, the complement to the 530 note is the linking entry field for a link to another format. This is the _____ field. 6.___

    A. 538   B. 776   C. 856   D. 949

7. What is the term for a complete revision of a Dewey Decimal class?

   A. Reconstruction
   B. Phoenix
   C. Rebridgement
   D. Overhaul

8. Which of the following network topologies tends to be faster and involve the least amount of cabling?

   A. Ring
   B. Matrix
   C. Bus
   D. Star

9. The method of choice for most libraries in authenticating access to electronic journals databases is

   A. User ID
   B. IP address
   C. Password
   D. User ID and password

10. Which of the following is one of S.R. Ranganathan's Five Laws of Library Science?

    A. The pen is mightier than the sword.
    B. Save the time of the reader.
    C. Every reader knows the book he/she wants to read already; it's just a matter of finding it.
    D. Information longs to be free.

11. The semantic relationship between the words "chapbook" and "pamphlet" is

    A. hierarchic
    B. locative
    C. associative
    D. synonymous

12. Which of the following is NOT a leading vendor of library management software?

    A. Logos
    B. Endeavor
    C. Auto-Graphics
    D. Sirsi

13. A systems librarian discovers old magnetic tapes in storage, which came from an obsolete computer system. The only way to read the data in the new library system is to write a special program. This method of bringing old data into new systems is referred to as data

    A. copying
    B. conversion
    C. reformatting
    D. migration

14. Which of the following is LEAST likely to be categorized as a social science?

    A. History
    B. Law
    C. Journalism
    D. Anthropology

15. What is the term for a classified display in a thesaurus of indexing terms that shows the complete hierarchy of descriptors, from the broadest to the most specific, usually by indention?

    A. Tree structure
    B. Indexing matrix
    C. Dichotomous key
    D. Cant

16. Which of the following storage media has the greatest storage capacity?

    A. ZIP disk
    B. CD-RW
    C. CD-ROM
    D. DVD-ROM

17. A _____ license with an electronic database publisher is a unilateral license who terms are accepted with the software package is opened.

    A. shrink-wrap
    B. force majeure
    C. click-wrap
    D. pay-per-view

18. One way to limit search results in Web search engines and directories is to use phrase searching, which involves

    A. using Boolean terms such as AND or NOT
    B. putting quotation marks around the search words
    C. putting parentheses around the search words
    D. putting an asterisk after the search words

19. In book sales, the largest discounts offered by publishers are typically _____ discounts.

    A. trade
    B. cash
    C. library
    D. convention

20. Reference software is NOT the most appropriate learning tool when users want to

    A. investigate topics that may be beyond their reading capabilities
    B. browse a number of topics
    C. learn how to perform a specific task
    D. ask a specific question

21. The holdings of all the libraries in a library system, in which libraries owning at least one copy of an item are identified by name and/or location symbol, are always accessible from the

    A. union catalog
    B. bibliographic database
    C. OPAC
    D. reference desk

21.____

22. An overview article on a particular topic is MOST likely to be found in a(n)

    A. encyclopedia
    B. index
    C. gazetteer
    D. dictionary

22.____

23. In the MARC record, the same digits are assigned across fields in the second and third character positions of the tag to indicate data of the same type. For example, tags reading "X51" contain information about

    A. personal names
    B. topical terms
    C. bibliographic titles
    D. geographic names

23.____

24. Generally, XML is NOT

    A. capable of storing context as well as content
    B. considered to be the optimal format for file compression and delivery
    C. able to display dynamic information as a document
    D. an excellent standard for business-to-business applications such as invoices and purchase orders

24.____

25. The USA Patriot Act provides that law enforcement agencies can compel libraries to
    I. produce circulation records
    II. provide Internet usage records
    III. remain silent about the existence of any warrants served on the library
    IV. reveal patron registration information

    A. I and II
    B. I, II and III
    C. II and III
    D. I, II, III and IV

25.____

KEY (CORRECT ANSWERS)

1. D
2. C
3. B
4. D
5. C

6. B
7. B
8. C
9. B
10. B

11. D
12. A
13. D
14. C
15. A

16. D
17. A
18. B
19. A
20. C

21. A
22. A
23. D
24. B
25. D

EXAMINATION SECTION
TEST 1

DIRECTIONS: Each question or incomplete statement is followed by several suggested answers or completions. Select the one that BEST answers the question or completes the statement. *PRINT THE LETTER OF THE CORRECT ANSWER IN THE SPACE AT THE RIGHT.*

Questions 1-5.

DIRECTIONS: Arrange the following names in alphabetical order as they would appear on the hold shelf of a library by matching the name in Column A with its order position in Column B.

Column A	Column B	
1. Smiles, Roy	A. First	1.____
2. Smigel, Robert	B. Second	2.____
	C. Third	
3. Smith, Raymond	D. Fourth	3.____
	E. Fifth	
4. Smith, Rhonda		4.____
5. Smiegel, Rayna		5.____

Questions 6-10.

DIRECTIONS: Each of Questions 6 through 10 may be:
    A. Incorrect due to improper spelling
    B. Incorrect due to improper punctuation
    C. Incorrect due to improper capitalization
    D. Correct

6. The reference section is non-circulating, this means you can't check these items out.   6.____

7. The book can be found in the non-ficton section of the library.   7.____

8. Biographies are a popular selection among all age groups at our library.   8.____

9. The elm grove library is the third biggest library in the county.   9.____

10. Since your book was one week overdue, I cannot wave this fine for you.   10.____

Questions 11-15.

DIRECTIONS: Questions 11 through 15 are to be answered SOLELY on the basis of the information given in the following paragraph.

Libraries have a long history, with the oldest recorded library dating back to Ancient Egypt circa 367 BC to 283 BC. In recent years, however, technological developments have changed the nature of library service. The rise of the internet and the growing number of digital libraries have resulted in a decrease in library usage. Throughout history, library service has primarily focused on the collection of books and other resources a library offers to its patrons. This collection-centered approach to library service has been challenged by the public's ability to access much of this information virtually without ever stepping inside of a library. Fortunately, there is another approach to library service that remains useful and relevant in the digital age: a user-centered approach. A user-centered approach shifts the focus from a library's physical collection to the services it provides to promote learning and social interaction among its users.

11. Based on what you've read in the above paragraph, which of the following would be an example of user-centered library service?
    A. A library's acquisition of a rare manuscript
    B. The expansion of a library's digital collection
    C. The installation of more shelving to house a larger and more diverse collection
    D. the creation of a librarian-led study group for adult learners returning to school

11.____

12. According to the above paragraph, libraries have been around for about _____ years.
    A. 500   B. 2,300   C. 1,700   D. 100

12.____

13. According to the above paragraph, what has made a collection-centered approach to library service less useful?
    A. Poor collection development   B. A decrease in book prices
    C. Technological advancements   D. A more educated public

13.____

14. Based on what you've read in the above paragraph, what must libraries do to remain relevant in the modern age?
    A. Adopt a user-centered approach to library service
    B. Adopt a collection-centered approach to library service
    C. Seek funding from new sources
    D. Abandon physical collections for completely digital collections

14.____

15. Based on what you've read in the above paragraph, which of the following BEST describes the difference between collection-centered and user-centered library service?
    Collection-centered library service focuses on _____, while user-centered library service focuses on _____.
    A. the services a library offers that promote learning and socialization; a library's physical holdings of books and resources
    B. digitizing a library's entire collection; maintaining a physical collection

15.____

C. maintaining a physical collection; digitizing a library's entire collection
D. a library's physical holdings of books and resources; the services a library offers that promote learning and socialization

Questions 16-20.

DIRECTIONS: Questions 16 through 20 each consist of four call numbers in Column A and Column B. Compare the numbers listed in each column and use the following to provide your answer:
A. One call number in Column A and Column B are the same
B. Two call numbers in Column A and Column B are the same
C. Three call numbers in Column A and Column B are the same
D. All four call numbers in Column A and Column B are the same

Column A	Column B	
16. 696.45 BAC 645.96 CAB 656.46 DAN 646.56 AND	696.45 CAB 645.96 BAC 656.46 DAN 646.56 AND	16.____
17. 251.84 NEJ 258.14 ENE 284.84 NEE 248.15 JEE	251.84 NEJ 258.14 ENE 284.84 NEE 248.15 JEE	17.____
18. 199.33 WEN 139.93 WEW 113.31 NEW 133.99 WEE	199.33 WEN 139.93 WEN 113.31 WEW 133.93 WEE	18.____
19. 823.65 HOW 832.56 WHO 862.35 WOW 856.23 WON	823.65 HOW 823.56 WHO 862.35 WOW 856.23 WON	19.____
20. 429.55 BEB 495.22 BEE 422.95 EBB 492.59 EBE	429.55 BEB 492.22 BEE 422.95 EBB 495.29 EBE	20.____

Questions 21-25.

DIRECTIONS: Questions 21 through 25 are to be answered on the basis of the following table.

Dry Creek Library Monthly Adult Program Records				
Program	Number of Attendees Ages 18-24	Number of Attendees Ages 25-44	Number of Attendees Ages 45-65	Number of Attendees Age 65+
Writers' Group	4	5	4	3
Knitting Circle	4	3	3	2
Tai Chi	3	4	1	6
Mystery Book Club	0	2	3	4
Non-Fiction Book Club	2	5	4	3

21. Which program has the HIGHEST attendance rate? 21.____
    A. Writers' Group   B. Tai Chi
    C. Non-Fiction Book Club   D. Knitting Circle

22. Which age group has the HIGHEST participation rate in monthly library 22.____
    programs?
    A. 18-24   B. 25-44   C. 45-65   D. 65+

23. Which program is MOST popular among 18 to 44 year olds? 23.____
    A. Writers' Group   B. Knitting Club
    C. Mystery Book Club   D. Non-Fiction Book Club

24. If the library were to discontinue a program, which program would be the 24.____
    MOST logical choice based upon these program records?
    A. Writers' Group   B. Tai Chi
    C. Mystery Book Club   D. Knitting Circle

25. If the library wants to expand one program from monthly to weekly in 25.____
    order to attract more seniors, which program would be the MOST logical choice
    based on these program records?
    A. Writers' Group   B. Knitting Circle
    C. Mystery Book Club   D. Tai Chi

KEY (CORRECT ANSWERS)

1.	C		11.	D
2.	B		12.	B
3.	D		13.	C
4.	E		14.	A
5.	A		15.	D
6.	B		16.	B
7.	A		17.	D
8.	D		18.	A
9.	C		19.	C
10.	A		20.	B

21. A
22. B
23. A
24. C
25. D

TEST 2

DIRECTIONS: Each question or incomplete statement is followed by several suggested answers or completions. Select the one that BEST answers the question or completes the statement. *PRINT THE LETTER OF THE CORRECT ANSWER IN THE SPACE AT THE RIGHT.*

1. Which of the following words is spelled INCORRECTLY? 1._____
   A. microfiche   B. photocopyer   C. interlibrary   D. catalog

2. Which of the following sentences includes an error in punctuation? 2._____
   A. I'm holding Mr. Rutgers book at the circulation desk.
   B. All meeting rooms are currently reserved.
   C. Only library cardholders can request books through interlibrary loan.
   D. Children's books are located upstairs in the Youth Services Department.

3. Which of the following sentences includes a capitalization error? 3._____
   A. The library director must sign off on all purchases.
   B. This week the Ashton Public Library Book Club is reading *The Paris Wife*.
   C. If you need help with academic research, you should speak with a librarian in the department of reference services.
   D. Our most popular program is our weekly Gourmet Club, where people come together to talk about fine food and drinks.

4. Which of the following words is spelled INCORRECTLY? 4._____
   A. biography   B. anthology   C. magizine   D. bibliography

5. Which of the following sentences includes an error in punctuation? 5._____
   A. Can I see your driver's license?
   B. Ms. Janda said that she would be arriving 10 minutes late for the computer class.
   C. There are only three copies left of the book selected for the monthly book club.
   D. Who did you speak to over the phone about this hold request.

Questions 6-10.

DIRECTIONS: Questions 6 through 10 include sentences with one word underlined. For each question, please select the word with the CLOSEST meaning to the underlined word.

6. Mr. Banks has a block on his account because he has too many <u>fines</u>. 6._____
   A. charges   B. items   C. warnings   D. restrictions

7. *The Girl With the Dragon Tattoo* received overwhelmingly positive <u>reviews</u>. 7._____
   A. investments   B. reassessments
   C. critiques   D. inspections

48

8. When you write a research paper, you must include citations. 8.____
   A. commendations B. references
   C. facts D. inferences

9. If you make a copy of that CD, you are infringing upon copyright law. 9.____
   A. preserving B. misunderstanding
   C. violating D. elucidating

10. *Architectural Digest* is located on the first floor with the other serials. 10.____
    A. books B. databases C. periodicals D. archives

Questions 11-15.

DIRECTIONS: Questions 11 through 15 consist of four addresses in Column A and Column B. Compare the addresses listed in each column and use the following to provide your answer:
   A. One address in Column A and Column B are the same.
   B. Two addresses in Column A and Column B are the same.
   C. Three addresses in Column A and Column B are the same.
   D. All four addresses in Column A and Column B are the same.

Column A	Column B	
11. 3941 Blackwell Dr. 3491 Blackwell Dr. 3991 Blackswell St. 3945 Blackstreet Ave.	3941 Blackwell Dr. 3914 Balckwell Dr. 3941 Blackwell St. 3945 Blackstreet Dr.	11.____
12. 204 Rhodes Ave. Apt. B 206 Rhodes Ave. Apt. 6 206 Rhoades Ave. Apt B 260 Rhodes St. Apt. B6	204 Rhodes Ave. Apt. B 204 Rhodes Ave. Apt 4 206 Rhoades Ave. Apt. B 260 Rhodes St. Apt. B6	12.____
13. 1155 Judith Rd. 1515 Judith Ln. 5111 Judy Rd. 1155 Judy Ln.	1155 Judith Rd. 1515 Judith Ln. 5111 Judy Rd. 1155 Judy Ln.	13.____
14. 2367 Cascade Blvd. 7632 Cascade Ave. 2367 Cascadia Blvd. 7632 Cascade Blvd.	2376 Cascade Blvd. 7632 Cascade Ave. 2367 Cascadia Blvd. 7632 Cascadia Blvd.	14.____
15. 106 Brooks Ln. Apt. 12 102 Brooks Ln. Apt. 16 126 Brook Ln. Apt. 11 162 Brook Ave. Apt. 2	106 Brooks Ln. Apt. 12 102 Brooks Ln. Apt. 16 126 Brooks Ln. Apt. 11 166 Brook Ave. Apt. 2	15.____

Questions 16-20.

DIRECTIONS: In Questions 16 through 20, please match the author's last name in Column A with its proper order on the shelf of a library that organizes fiction alphabetically by author's last name in Column B.

Column A	Column B	
16. Brockenstein	A. First	16._____
17. Brock	B. Second	17._____
	C. Third	
18. Broadchurch	D. Fourth	18._____
	E. Fifth	
19. Broadbent		19._____
20. Brockley		20._____

21. If a patron returns five books two days past their due date, and overdue charges accrue at 15 cents per day for each book, how much does the patron owe in overdue fees?
    A. $1.50   B. $0.75   C. $3.00   D. $5.75

22. Susan is compiling statistics from monthly library usage records. Records state that over the course of one month, patrons checked out 5,375 adult fiction titles, 4,789 adult non-fiction titles, 6,854 audio-visual items, and 3,632 magazines. Based on these records, fiction titles comprise about _____ percent of overall monthly circulation.
    A. 52   B. 26   C. 15   D. 38

23. Yearly statistics show that over the course of one week an average of 33 patrons attend library programs. If there are four programs scheduled during one week, about how many patrons will be attending each program?
    A. 3   B. 11   C. 5   D. 8

24. Jane is calling patrons to inform them that the interlibrary loan books they requested have arrived. It takes Jane approximately five minutes to notify each patron, and she has a cart filled with 37 interlibrary books that require patron notification. She also has a bin full of returned books that need to be checked in and shelved. How long will it take Jane to finish the hold notifications so she can move on to her next task?
    A. One hour   B. About six hours
    C. About three hours   D. 45 minutes

25. Birch Grove Library has a rule that patrons can only check out 50 books at a time, 50 audio-visual items at a time, and 15 interlibrary loan items at a time. The library also has a rule that no more than 75 items total can be checked out to a patron's account at one time. If a patron already has 45 books, 25 audio-visual items, and 5 interlibrary loan items checked out, she can

    A. still check out 5 books, 25 audio-visual items, 5 interlibrary loan items
    B. no longer check anything out until she returns some of her items
    C. still check out 30 books
    D. still check out 10 interlibrary loan items and 25 audio-visual items

25._____

KEY (CORRECT ANSWERS)

1. B
2. A
3. C
4. C
5. D

11. A
12. C
13. D
14. B
15. B

6. A
7. C
8. B
9. C
10. C

16. D
17. C
18. B
19. A
20. E

21. A
22. B
23. D
24. C
25. B

TEST 3

DIRECTIONS: Each question or incomplete statement is followed by several suggested answers or completions. Select the one that BEST answers the question or completes the statement. *PRINT THE LETTER OF THE CORRECT ANSWER IN THE SPACE AT THE RIGHT.*

Questions 1-5.

DIRECTIONS: Questions 1 through 5 are to be answered on the basis of the following paragraph.

Copyright law plays an important role in how libraries operate and provide information to their patrons. Libraries must abide by state and federal copyright laws, including the Copyright Act, which is the most authoritative source of copyright law in the United States. Through the Copyright Act's first sale doctrine, libraries are allowed to lend books and other copyrighted material. Additionally, the Copyright Act's fair use law allows library patrons to use copyrighted materials for specific functions, such as criticism, comment, news reporting, scholarship, and research. Copyright law also allows libraries to reproduce copyrighted works in order to preserve or replace these works or provide them to people with disabilities.

1. Which of the following would NOT be an acceptable reason for a library to reproduce copyrighted material?
   A. To deliver it to a person who is housebound due to a physical disability
   B. To sell it in the library's book sale in order to raise funds for the library's remodel
   C. To preserve a book that is currently out of print and that also has limited used copies available
   D. To replace a copy of a rare book that has been lost

2. Which law allows libraries to lend books and other copyrighted materials?
   A. This is not allowed under state or federal law
   B. The fair use law
   C. The first sale doctrine
   D. The first use act

3. Based on the fair use law, libraries can allow patrons to quote or use passages from copyrighted materials in
   A. newspaper articles
   B. business brochures
   C. book manuscripts set for publication
   D. television advertisements

4. In the United States, copyright law PRIMARILY comes from
   A. state law
   B. the first use act
   C. municipal law
   D. the Copyright Act

1.____

2.____

3.____

4.____

5. The fair use law can be found in
   A. state law
   B. the Copyright Act
   C. the First Amendment
   D. municipal law

   5._____

6. Which of the following words is spelled INCORRECTLY?
   A. alamnac   B. dictionary   C. atlas   D. encyclopedia

   6._____

7. Which of the following sentences contains an error in punctuation?
   A. There are two titles on hold for members of the library's book club: *Gone Girl* and *Me Before You*.
   B. At the beginning of each month the library director holds a staff meeting that everyone is required to attend.
   C. Did you ask the patron for her photo I.D. before providing her with her account information?
   D. The library's Knitting Circle meets the first Thursday, second Saturday and third Monday of every month.

   7._____

8. Which of the following words is spelled INCORRECTLY?
   A. classification   B. plagarism   C. withdrawn   D. volume

   8._____

9. Which of the following sentences includes an error in capitalization?
   A. All of the items you had on hold were sent back Tuesday.
   B. Did Mr. Phekos register for this week's cooking demonstration?
   C. Tanner is helping with the fundraiser because he is a member of the friends of the library.
   D. Book donations can be placed in the donation box near the circulation desk.

   9._____

10. Which of the following words is spelled INCORRECTLY?
    A. thesarus   B. thesis   C. series   D. reserve

    10._____

Questions 11-15.

DIRECTIONS: Questions 11 through 15 each contain three lines of letters in Column A and three lines of numbers in Column B. The letters in each line should correspond with the numbers in each line as outlined in the following table:

Letter	J	R	D	T	M	C	P	K	O	S
Matching Number	0	1	2	3	4	5	6	7	8	9

Please answer the questions as follows:
A. None of the lines of letters and lines of numbers are matched correctly.
B. One of the lines of letters and numbers is matched correctly.
C. Two of the lines of letters and lines of numbers are matched correctly.
D. All three of the lines of letters and lines of numbers are matched correctly.

Column A	Column B
11. JMCP	0456
RMKS	1479
CPRO	5618
12. DRKS	9172
MKPJ	4761
JDCP	0256
13. CSDJ	5924
RKRD	1712
JKPC	0765
14. TMMO	3448
CPDR	5632
JOTS	0839
15. JCMS	0648
ROST	1983
MKJD	4701

11.____

12.____

13.____

14.____

15.____

Questions 16-20.

DIRECTIONS: In Questions 16 through 20, match the book title in Column A with its proper alphabetical orders based on letter by letter filing rules.

Column A	Column B
16. To Kill a Mockingbird	A. First
	B. Second
17. A Tale of Two Cities	C. Third
	D. Fourth
18. The Time Traveler's Wife	E. Fifth
19. Treasure Island	
20. The Two Towers	

16.____

17.____

18.____

19.____

20.____

Questions 21-25.

DIRECTIONS: Questions 21 through 25 are to be answered on the basis of the following table.

Dry Creek Library 2023 Library Card Registration by Season					
Season	Number of Registrants Under 18	Number of Registrants Ages 18-24	Number of Registrants Ages 25-44	Number of Registrants Ages 45-65	Number of Registrants Age 65+
Winter	56	34	69	48	34
Spring	72	47	55	62	48
Summer	100	75	71	89	101
Fall	96	115	88	72	63

21. During which season does Dry Creek Library experience the MOST library card registrations?
    A. Winter
    B. Spring
    C. Summer
    D. Fall

22. Which of the following age groups registered for the MOST library cards in 2023?
    A. Under 18
    B. 18-24
    C. 25-44
    D. 45-65

23. Which of the following patrons is MOST likely to register for a library card in the fall based on the data shown in the above table?
    A. A 10-year-old preparing for the new school year
    B. A 65-year-old who has just retired from his full-time job
    C. An 18-year-old entering her first semester of college
    D. A 26-year-old enrolled in medical school

24. During which season should Dry Creek Library increase marketing efforts to draw in more registrants between the ages of 18 and 24?
    A. Winter
    B. Spring
    C. Summer
    D. Fall

25. In 2022, 1,364 people registered for new library cards. How does this number compare to the number of registrants in 2023?
    It is _____ registered in 2023.
    A. the same amount of people that
    B. slightly less than the number of people who
    C. significantly more than the number of people who
    D. significantly less than the number of people who

KEY (CORRECT ANSWERS)

1. B
2. C
3. A
4. D
5. B

6. A
7. B
8. B
9. C
10. A

11. D
12. B
13. C
14. C
15. A

16. C
17. A
18. B
19. D
20. E

21. C
22. A
23. C
24. A
25. B

TEST 4

DIRECTIONS: Each question or incomplete statement is followed by several suggested answers or completions. Select the one that BEST answers the question or completes the statement. *PRINT THE LETTER OF THE CORRECT ANSWER IN THE SPACE AT THE RIGHT.*

Questions 1-5.

DIRECTIONS: Each of the sentences provided in Questions 1 through 5 may be:
- A. Incorrect due to improper spelling
- B. Incorrect due to improper punctuation
- C. Incorrect due to improper capitalization
- D. Correct

1. When you search the library's catalog online you can search by author, title, subject or, keyword.   1.____

2. The movie "Ghostbusters" is available on DVD or Blu-Ray in the library's audiovisual department.   2.____

3. The library hosts a group for writers that meets monthly and a children's story hour that meets weekly.   3.____

4. Reference librarians are best equipped to answer questions about the library's electronic resorces.   4.____

5. Library patrons can sign into their library account online to pay fines, rezerve books and check their due dates.   5.____

Questions 6-10.

DIRECTIONS: Questions 6 through 10 include sentences with one word underlined. Please select the word with the CLOSEST meaning to the underlined word.

6. The patron has <u>requested</u> that the book be held for an extra two days because she is on vacation.   6.____
 - A. refused   B. asked   C. determined   D. stated

7. The Oak Creek Village Library participates in a <u>reciprocal</u> borrowing program in which it shares library materials with 25 other libraries.   7.____
 - A. individual
 - B. restrictive
 - C. collaborative
 - D. bibliographic

8. In libraries, books are assigned a call number based upon the book's <u>subject</u>.   8.____
 - A. title   B. author   C. chronology   D. topic

9. Every year, the library director and board of directors review and update library policies.
   A. procedures   B. collections   C. events   D. affairs

10. Librarians at the Poplar Lane Library are sometimes asked to proctor official tests and exams.
    A. barter   B. supervise   C. process   D. create

Questions 11-15.

DIRECTIONS: In answering Questions 11 through 15, arrange the following names in alphabetical order as they would appear on the hold shelf of a library by matching the name in Column A with its order position in Column B.

Column A

11. Frey, James
12. Friend, Jayne
13. Frye, Jada
14. Friel, Jewel
15. Frillo, Juno

Column B
A. First
B. Second
C. Third
D. Fourth
E. Fifth

Questions 16-20.

DIRECTIONS: Questions 16 through 20 each consist of four call numbers in Column A and Column B. Compare the numbers listed in each column and use the following to provide your answer:
A. One call number in Column A and Column B are the same.
B. Two call numbers in Column A and Column B are the same.
C. Three call numbers in Column A and Column B are the same.
D. All four call numbers in Column A and Column B are the same.

	Column A	Column B
16.	147.74CAL 174.47LAC 144.77LAL 411.77CAC	147.74CAL 174.44LAC 177.44LAL 477.11CAL
17.	467.09DAN 469.07DAD 460.79NAD 468.32DAJ	467.09DAN 469.07DAD 460.79NAD 468.23DAJ

18. 219.57KAR   219.57KAR   18.____
     215.97KAR   215.57KAR
     257.19RAR   257.19RAR
     275.19KAK   275.19KAK

19. 112.48PAU   112.58PAU   19.____
     112.85PUA   112.85PUA
     124.18PUL   124.18PUL
     142.85PAU   142.85PAA

20. 102.75CHR   102.75CHR   20.____
     175.27CRI   175.27CRI
     107.25CHR   107.25CHR
     157.22CRI   157.22CRI

21. Old Towne Library is hosting a speaking event and book signing with a   21.____
    well-known author. Seats are available for 120 people, but the author only has
    one hour to sign books afterward. If it takes about three minutes to sign each
    person's book, how many of the event's attendees will be able to participate in
    the book signing?
    A. All of them   B. 20   C. 100   D. 50

22. If Fleetwood Library owns a total of 1,000 DVDs (500 in the fiction section and   22.____
    500 in the non-fiction section), how many DVDs would the library have left if the
    library director decided to withdraw 120 fiction DVDs and 150 non-fiction DVDs,
    while simultaneously adding 75 fiction DVDs and 60 non-fiction DVDs?
    A. 730   B. 805   C. 865   D. 950

23. Tandy has been asked to create the schedule for the circulation staff at   23.____
    Morton Pass Library. The library is open from 10 A.M. to 9 P.M. Monday
    through Friday, from 10 A.M. to 5 P.M. on Saturday, and from 12 P.M. to 5 P.M.
    on Sunday. The library director requires that two staff members work at the
    desk during all hours of operation. What is the TOTAL number of hours Tandy
    will need to schedule staff for next week's schedule?
    A. 134   B. 55   C. 201   D. 68

24. The Boynton Canyon Library hosts a weekly book discussion group every   24.____
    Thursday night. If 8 people attended the group the first week of February, 11
    attended the second week, 7 attended the third week, and 10 attended the
    fourth week, what is the average number of attendees for the month of
    February?
    A. 9   B. 34   C. 10   D. 7

25. A library patron has $6.60 in fines on his library account. He returns five more books five days late and is charged $.15 a day for each book. The library does not let patrons check out library materials when the fines on their account exceed $10.00. Which of the following statements BEST describes the patron's current situation?
   The patron
   A. has less than $10.00 in fines and can still check out library materials
   B. must pay at least $1.00 in fines before he can check out more library materials
   C. must pay at least $.60 in fines before he can check out more library materials
   D. must pay at least $.35 in fines before he can check out more library materials

25.____

KEY (CORRECT ANSWERS)

1. B
2. C
3. D
4. A
5. A

6. B
7. C
8. D
9. A
10. B

11. A
12. C
13. E
14. B
15. D

16. A
17. C
18. C
19. B
20. D

21. B
22. C
23. A
24. A
25. D

RECORD KEEPING
EXAMINATION SECTION
TEST 1

DIRECTIONS: Each question or incomplete statement is followed by several suggested answers or completions. Select the one that BEST answers the question or completes the statement. *PRINT THE LETTER OF THE CORRECT ANSWER IN THE SPACE AT THE RIGHT.*

Questions 1-15.

DIRECTIONS: Questions 1 through 15 are to be answered on the basis of the following list of company names below. Arrange a file alphabetically, word-by-word, disregarding punctuation, conjunctions, and apostrophes. Then answer the questions.

    A Bee C Reading Materials
    ABCO Parts
    A Better Course for Test Preparation
    AAA Auto Parts Co.
    A-Z Auto Parts, Inc.
    Aabar Books
    Abbey, Joanne
    Boman-Sylvan Law Firm
    BMW Autowerks
    C Q Service Company
    Chappell-Murray, Inc.
    E&E Life Insurance
    Emcrisco
    Gigi Arts
    Gordon, Jon & Associates
    SOS Plumbing
    Schmidt, J.B. Co.

1. Which of these files should appear FIRST?   1.____
   A. ABCO Parts
   B. A Bee C Reading Materials
   C. A Better Course for Test Preparation
   D. AAA Auto Parts Co.

2. Which of these files should appear SECOND?   2.____
   A. A-Z Auto Parts, Inc.
   B. A Bee C Reading Materials
   C. A Better Course for Test Preparation
   D. AAA Auto Parts Co.

2 (#1)

3. Which of these files should appear THIRD? 3.____
   A. ABCO Parts
   B. A Bee C Reading Materials
   C. Aabar Books
   D. AAA Auto Parts Co.

4. Which of these files should appear FOURTH? 4.____
   A. Aabar Books
   B. ABCO Parts
   C. Abbey, Joanne
   D. AAA Auto Parts Co.

5. Which of these files should appear LAST? 5.____
   A. Gordon, Jon & Associates
   B. Gigi Arts
   C. Schmidt, J.B. Co.
   D. SOS Plumbing

6. Which of these files should appear between A-Z Auto Parts, Inc. and Abbey, Joanne? 6.____
   A. A Bee C Reading Materials
   B. AAA Auto Parts Co.
   C. ABCO Parts
   D. A Better Course for Test Preparation

7. Which of these files should appear between ABCO Parts and Aabar Books? 7.____
   A. A Bee C Reading Materials
   B. Abbey, Joanne
   C. Aabar Books
   D. A-Z Auto Parts

8. Which of these files should appear between Abbey, Joanne and Boman-Sylvan Law Firm? 8.____
   A. A Better Course for Test Preparation
   B. BMW Autowerks
   C. Chappell-Murray, Inc.
   D. Aabar Books

9. Which of these files should appear between Abbey, Joanne and C Q Service? 9.____
   A. A-Z Auto Parts, Inc.
   B. BMW Autowerks
   C. Choices A and B
   D. Chappell-Murray, Inc.

10. Which of these files should appear between C Q Service Company and Emcrisco? 10.____
    A. Chappell-Murray, Inc.
    B. E&E Life Insurance
    C. Gigi Arts
    D. Choices A and B

11. Which of these files should NOT appear between C Q Service Company and E&E Life Insurance? 11.____
    A. Gordon, Jon & Associates
    B. Emcrisco
    C. Gigi Arts
    D. All of the above

12. Which of these files should appear between Chappell-Murray, Inc. and 12.____
    Gigi Arts?
    A. C Q Service Inc., E&E Life Insurance, and Emcrisco
    B. Emcrisco, E&E Life Insurance, and Gordon, Jon & Associates
    C. E&E Life Insurance, and Emcrisco
    D. Emcrisco and Gordon, Jon & Associates

13. Which of these files should appear between Gordon, Jon & Associates and 13.____
    SOS Plumbing?
    A. Gigi Arts   B. Schmidt, J.B. Co.
    C. Choices A and B   D. None of the above

14. Each of the choices lists the four files in their proper alphabetical order 14.____
    EXCEPT
    A. E&E Life Insurance; Gigi Arts; Gordon, Jon & Associates; SOS Plumbing
    B. E&E Life Insurance; Emcrisco; Gigi Arts; SOS Plumbing
    C. Emcrisco; Gordon, Jon & Associates; SOS Plumbing; Schmidt, J.B. Co.
    D. Emcrisco; Gigi Arts; Gordon, Jon & Associates; SOS Plumbing

15. Which of the choices lists the four files in their proper alphabetical order? 15.____
    A. Gigi Arts; Gordon, Jon & Associates; SOS Plumbing; Schmidt, J.B. Co.
    B. Gordon, Jon & Associates; Gigi Arts; Schmidt, J.B. Co.; SOS Plumbing
    C. Gordon, Jon & Associates; Gigi Arts; SOS Plumbing; Schmidt, J.B. Co.
    D. Gigi Arts; Gordon, Jon & Associates; Schmidt, J.B. Co.; SOS Plumbing

16. The alphabetical filing order of two businesses with identical names is 16.____
    determined by the
    A. length of time each business has been operating
    B. addresses of the businesses
    C. last name of the company president
    D. no one of the above

17. In an alphabetical filing system, if a business name includes a number, it should 17.____
    be
    A. disregarded
    B. considered a number and placed at the end of an alphabetical section
    C. treated as though it were written in words and alphabetized accordingly
    D. considered a number and placed at the beginning of an alphabetical
       section

18. If a business name includes a contraction (such as *don't* or *it's*), how should 18.____
    that word be treated in an alphabetical system?
    A. Divide the word into its separate parts and treat it as two words
    B. Ignore the letters that come after the apostrophe
    C. Ignore the word that contains the contraction
    D. Ignore the apostrophe and consider all letters in the contraction

19. In what order should the parts of an address be considered when using an alphabetical filing system?
    A. City or town; state; street name; house or building number
    B. State; city or town; street name; house or building number
    C. House or building number; street name; city or town; state
    D. Street name; city or town; state

20. A business record should be cross-referenced when a(n)
    A. organization is known by an abbreviated name
    B. business has a name change because of a sale, incorporation, or other reason
    C. business is known by a *coined* or common name which differs from a dictionary spelling
    D. all of the above

21. A geographical filing system is MOST effective when
    A. location is more important than name
    B. many names or titles sound alike
    C. dealing with companies who have offices all over the world
    D. filing personal and business files

Questions 22-25.

DIRECTIONS: Questions 22 through 25 are to be answered on the basis of the list of items below, which are to be filed geographically. Organize the items geographically and then answer the questions.

    I. University Press at Berkeley, U.S.
    II. Maria Sanchez, Mexico City, Mexico
    III. Great Expectations Ltd. in London, England
    IV. Justice League, Cape Town, South Africa, Africa
    V. Crown Pearls Ltd. in London, England
    VI. Joseph Prasad in London, England

22. Which of the following arrangements of the items is composed according to the policy of: *Continent, Country, City, Firm or Individual Name*?
    A. V, III, IV, VI, II, I
    B. IV, V, III, VI, II, I
    C. I, IV, V, III, VI, II
    D. IV, V, III, VI, I, II

23. Which of the following files is arranged according to the policy of: *Continent, Country, City, Firm or Individual Name*?
    A. South Africa; Africa; Cape Town; Justice League
    B. Mexico; Mexico City; Maria Sanchez
    C. North America; United States; Berkeley; University Press
    D. England; Europe; London; Prasad, Joseph

24. Which of the following arrangements of the items is composed according to the   24.____
    policy of: *Country, City, Firm or Individual Name*?
    A. V, VI, III, II, IV, I   B. I, V, VI, III, II, IV
    C. VI, V, III, II, IV, I   D. V, III, VI, II, IV, I

25. Which of the following files is arranged according to a policy of: *Country,*   25.____
    City, Firm or Individual Name?
    A. England; London; Crown Pearls Ltd.
    B. North America; United States; Berkeley; University Press
    C. Africa; Cape Town; Justice League
    D. Mexico City; Mexico; Maria Sanchez

26. Under which of the following circumstances would a phonetic filing system be   26.____
    MOST effective?
    A. When the person in charge of filing can't spell very well
    B. With large files with names that sound alike
    C. With large files with names that are spelled alike
    D. All of the above

Questions 27-29.

DIRECTIONS: Questions 27 through 29 are to be answered on the basis of the following list of
             numerical files.

             I.   391-023-100
             II. 361-132-170
             III. 385-732-200
             IV. 381-432-150
             V.   391-632-387
             VI. 361-423-303
             VII. 391-123-271

27. Which of the following arrangements of the files follows a consecutive-digit   27.____
    system?
    A. II, III, IV, I   B. I, V, VII, III   C. II, IV, III, I   D. III, I, V, VII

28. Which of the following arrangements follows a terminal-digit system?   28.____
    A. I, VII, II, IV, III   B. II, I, IV, V, VII
    C. VII, VI, V, IV, III   D. I, IV, II, III, VII

29. Which of the following lists follows a middle-digit system?   29.____
    A. I, VII, II, VI, IV, V, III   B. I, II, VII, IV, VI, V, III
    C. VII, II, I, III, V, VI, IV   D. VII, I, II, IV, VI, V, III

Questions 30-31.

DIRECTIONS: Questions 30 and 31 are to be answered on the basis of the following information.

 I. Reconfirm Laura Bates appointment with James Caldecort on December 12 at 9:30 A.M.
 II. Laurence Kinder contact Julia Lucas on August 3 and set up a meeting for week of September 23 at 4 P.M.
 III. John Lutz contact Larry Waverly on August 3 and set up appointment for September 23 at 9:30 A.M.
 IV. Call for tickets for Gerry Stanton August 21 for New Jersey on September 23, flight 143 at 4:43 P.M.

30. A chronological file for the above information would be 30.____
 A. IV, III, II, I   B. III, II, IV, I   C. IV, II, III, I   D. III, I, II, IV

31. Using the above information, a chronological file for the date September 23 would be 31.____
 A. II, III, IV   B. III, I, IV   C. III, II, IV   D. IV, III, II

Questions 32-34.

DIRECTIONS: Questions 32 through 34 are to be answered on the basis of the following information.

 I. Call Roger Epstein, Ashoke Naipaul, Jon Anderson, and Sara Washingon on April 19 at 1:00 P.M. to set up meeting with Alika D'Ornay for June 6 in New York.
 II. Call Martin Ames before noon on April 19 to confirm afternoon meeting with Bob Greenwood on April 20th.
 III. Set up meeting room at noon for 2:30 P.M. meeting on April 19th.
 IV. Ashley Stanton contact Bob Greenwood at 9:00 A.M. on April 20 and set up meeting for June 6 at 8:30 A.M.
 V. Carol Guiland contact Shelby Van Ness during afternoon of April 20 and set up meeting for June 6 at 10:00 A.M.
 VI. Call airline and reserve tickets on June 6 for Roger Epstein trip to Denver on July 8.
 VII. Meeting at 2:30 P.M. on April 19th.

32. A chronological file for all of the above information would be 32.____
 A. II, I, III, VII, V, IV, VI   B. III, VII, II, I, IV, V, VI
 C. III, VII, I, II, V, IV, VI   D. II, III, I, VII, IV, V, VI

33. A chronological file for the date of April 19th would be 33.____
 A. II, III, VII, I   B. II, III, I, VII   C. VII, I, III, II   D. III, VII, I, II

34. Add the following information to the file, and then create a chronological file for April 20th: VIII. April 20: 3:00 P.M. meeting between Bob Greenwood and Martin Ames. 34.____
    A. IV, V, VIII   B. IV, VIII, V   C. VIII, V, IV   D. V, IV, VIII

35. The PRIMARY advantage of computer records over a manual system is 35.____
    A. speed of retrieval   B. accuracy
    C. cost   D. potential file loss

KEY (CORRECT ANSWERS)

1. B	11. D	21. A	31. C
2. C	12. C	22. B	32. D
3. D	13. B	23. C	33. B
4. A	14. C	24. D	34. A
5. D	15. D	25. A	35. A
6. C	16. B	26. B	
7. B	17. C	27. C	
8. B	18. D	28. D	
9. C	19. A	29. A	
10. D	20. D	30. B	

NAME AND NUMBER CHECKING
EXAMINATION SECTION
TEST 1

DIRECTIONS: This test is designed to measure your speed/and accuracy. You are urged to work both quickly and accurately and to do correctly as many lists as you can in the time allowed. The test consists of lists or pairs of names and numbers. Count the number of IDENTICAL pairs in each list. Then, select the correct number, 1, 2, 3, 4, 5, and indicate your choice in the space at the right. Two sample questions are presented for your guidance, together with the correct solutions.

SAMPLE LIST A
Adelphi College   – Adelphia College
Braxton Corp   – Braxeton Corp.
Wassaic State School   – Wassaic State School
Central Islip State Hospital   – Central Isllip State Hospital
Greenwich House   – Greenwich House

NOTE: There are only two correct pairs—Wassaic State School and Greenwich House. Therefore, the CORRECT answer is 2.

SAMPLE LIST B
78453694	– 78453684
784530	– 784530
533	– 534
67845	– 67845
2368745	– 2368755

NOTE: There are only two correct pairs—784530 and 67845. Therefore, the CORRECT answer is 2.

LIST 1   1.____
     98654327   - 98654327
     74932564   - 7492564
     61438652   - 61438652
     01297653   - 01287653
     1865439765   - 1865439765

LIST 2   2.____
     478362   - 478363
     278354792   - 278354772
     9327   - 9327
     297384625   - 27384625
     6428156   - 6428158

LIST 3
    Abbey House — Abbey House
    Actor's Fund Home — Actor's Fund Home
    Adrian Memorial — Adrian Memorial
    A. Clayton Powell Home — Clayton Powell House
    Abbot E. Kittredge Club — Abbott E. Kitteredge Club

3._____

LIST 4
    3682 — 3692
    21937453829 — 31927453829
    723 — 733
    2763920 — 2763920
    47293 — 47293

4._____

LIST 5
    Adra House — Adra House
    Adolescents' Court — Adolescents' Court
    Cliff Villa — Cliff Villa
    Clark Neighborhood House — Clark Neighborhood House
    Alma Mathews House — Alma Mathews House

5._____

LIST 6
    28734291 — 28734271
    63810263849 — 63810263846
    26831027 — 26831027
    368291 — 368291
    7238102637 — 7238102637

6._____

LIST 7
    Albion State T.S. — Albion State T.C.
    Clara de Hirsch Home — Clara De Hirsch Home
    Alice Carrington Royce — Alice Carington Royce
    Alice Chopin Nursery — Alice Chapin Nursery
    Lighthouse Eye Clinic — Lighthouse Eye Clinic

7._____

LIST 8
    327 — 329
    712438291026 — 712438291026
    2753829142 — 275382942
    826287 — 826289
    26435162839 — 26435162839

8._____

LIST 9
    Letchworth Village — Letchworth Village
    A.A.A.E. Inc. — A.A.A.E. Inc.
    Clear Pool Camp — Clear Pool Camp
    A.M.M.L.A. Inc. — A.M.M.L.A. Inc.
    J.G. Harbard — J.G. Harbord

9._____

3 (#1)

LIST 10   10._____
    8254   - 8256
    2641526   - 2641526
    4126389012   - 4126389102
    725   - 725
    76253917287   - 76253917287

LIST 11   11._____
    Attica State Prison   - Attica State Prison
    Nellie Murrah   - Nellie Murrah
    Club Marshall   - Club Marshal
    Assissium Casea-Maria - Assissium Casa-Maria
    The Homestead   - The Homestead

LIST 12   12._____
    2691   - 2691
    623819253627   - 623819253629
    28637   - 28937
    278392736   - 278392736
    52739   - 52739

LIST 13   13._____
    A.I.C.P. Boys Camp   - A.I.C.P. Boy's Camp
    Einar Chrystie   - Einar Christyie
    Astoria Center   - Astoria Center
    G. Frederick Brown   - G. Federick Browne
    Vacation Service   - Vacation Services

LIST 14   14._____
    728352689   - 728352688
    643728   - 643728
    37829176   - 37827196
    8425367   - 8425369
    65382018   - 65382018

LIST 15   15._____
    E.S. Streim   - E.S. Strim
    Charles E. Higgins   - Charles E. Higgins
    Baluvelt, N.Y.   - Blauwelt, N.Y.
    Roberta Magdalen   - Roberto Magdalen
    Ballard School   - Ballard School

LIST 16   16._____
    7382   - 7392
    281374538299   - 291374538299
    623   - 633
    6273730   - 6273730
    63392   - 63392

LIST 17
    Orrin Otis   - Orrin Otis
    Barat Settlement   - Barat Settlemen
    Emmanuel House   - Emmanuel House
    William T. McCreery   - William T. McCreery
    Seamen's Home   - Seaman's Home

17.____

LIST 18
    72824391   - 72834371
    3729106237   - 37291106237
    82620163849   - 82620163846
    37638921   - 37638921
    82631027   - 82631027

18.____

LIST 19
    Commonwealth Fund   - Commonwealth Fund
    Anne Johnsen   - Anne Johnson
    Bide-A-Wee Home   - Bide-a-Wee Home
    Riverdale-on-Hudson - Riverdal-on-Hudson
    Bialystoker Home   - Bailystoker Home

19.____

LIST 20
    9271   - 9271
    392918352627   - 392018852629
    72637   - 72637
    927392736   - 927392736
    92739   - 92739

20.____

LIST 21
    Charles M. Stump   - Charles M. Stump
    Bourne Workshop   - Buorne Workshop
    B'nai Bi'rith   - B'nai Brith
    Poppenhuesen Institute - Poppenheusen Institute
    Consular Service   - Consular Service

21.____

LIST 22
    927352689   - 927352688
    647382   - 648382
    93729176   - 93727196
    649536718   - 649536718
    5835367   - 5835369

22.____

LIST 23
    L.S. Bestend   - L.S. Bestent
    Hirsch Mfg. Co.   - Hircsh Mfg. Co.
    F.H. Storrs   - F.P. Storrs
    Camp Wassaic   - Camp Wassaic
    George Ballingham   - George Ballingham

23.____

5 (#1)

LIST 24
    372846392048   - 372846392048
    334   - 334
    7283524678   - 7283524678
    7283   - 7283
    7283629372   - 7283629372

24.____

LIST 25
    Dr. Stiles Company   - Dr. Stills Company
    Frances Hunsdon   - Frances Hunsdon
    Northrop Barrert   - Nothrup Barrent
    J.D. Brunjes   - J.D. Brunjes
    Theo. Claudel & Co.   - Theo. Claudel co.

25.____

KEY (CORRECT ANSWERS)

1.	3		11.	3
2.	1		12.	3
3.	2		13.	1
4.	2		14.	2
5.	5		15.	2
6.	3		16.	2
7.	1		17.	3
8.	2		18.	2
9.	4		19.	2
10.	3		20.	4

21. 2
22. 1
23. 2
24. 5
25. 2

TEST 2

DIRECTIONS: This test is designed to measure your speed/and accuracy. You are urged to work both quickly and accurately and to do correctly as many lists as you can in the time allowed. The test consists of lists or pairs of names and numbers. Count the number of IDENTICAL pairs in each list. Then, select the correct number, 1, 2, 3, 4, 5, and indicate your choice in the space at the right.

LIST 1
    82728   - 82738
    82736292637   - 82736292639
    728   - 738
    83926192527   - 83726192529
    82736272   - 82736272

1.____

LIST 2
    L. Pietri   - L. Pietri
    Mathewson, L.F.   - Mathewson, L.F.
    Funk & Wagnall   - Funk & Wagnalls
    Shimizu, Sojio   - Shimizu, Sojio
    Filing Equipment Bureau - Filing Equipment Buraeu

2.____

LIST 3
    63801829374   - 63801839474
    283577657   - 283577657
    65689   - 65689
    3457892026   - 3547893026
    2779   - 2778

3.____

LIST 4
    August Caille   - August Caille
    The Well-Fare Service   - The Wel-Fare Service
    K.L.M. Process co.   - R.L.M. Process Co.
    Merrill Littell   - Merrill Littell
    Dodd & Sons   - Dodd & Son

4.____

LIST 5
    998745732   - 998745733
    723   - 723
    463849102983   - 463849102983
    8570   - 8570
    279012   - 279012

5.____

LIST 6
    M.A. Wender   - M.A. Winder
    Minneapolis Supply Co. - Minneapolis Supply Co.
    Beverly Hills Corp   - Beverley Hills Corp.
    Trafalgar Square   - Trafalgar Square
    Phifer, D.T.   - Phiefer, D.T.

6.____

2 (#2)

LIST 7   7._____
    7834629   - 7834629
    3549806746   - 3549806746
    97802564   - 97892564
    689246   - 688246
    2578024683   - 2578024683

LIST 8   8._____
    Scadrons'   - Scadrons'
    Gensen & Bro.   - Genson & Bro.
    Firestone Co.   - Firestone Co.
    H.L. Eklund   - H.L. Eklund
    Oleomargarine Co.   - Oleomargarine Co.

LIST 9   9._____
    782039485618   - 782039485618
    53829172639   - 63829172639
    892   - 892
    82937482   - 829374820
    52937456   - 53937456

LIST 10   10._____
    First Nat'l Bank   - First Nat'l Bank
    Sedgwick Machine Works - Sedgewick Machine Works
    Hectographia Co.   - Hectographia Corp.
    Levet Bros.   - Levet Bros.
    Multistamp Co., Inc.   - Multistamp Co., Inc.

LIST 11   11._____
    7293   - 7293
    6382910293   - 6382910292
    981928374012   - 981928374912
    58293   - 58393
    18203649271   - 283019283745

LIST 12   12._____
    Lowrey Lb'r Co.   - Lowrey Lb'r Co.
    Fidelity Service   - Fidelity Service
    Reumann, J.A.   - Reumann, J.A.
    Duophoto Ltd.   - Duophotos Ltd.
    John Jarratt   - John Jaratt

LIST 13   13._____
    6820384   - 6820384
    383019283745   - 383019283745
    63927102   - 63928102
    91029354829   - 91029354829
    58291728   - 58291728

LIST 14
- Standard Press Co.   - Standard Press Co.
- Reliant Mf'g. Co.   - Relant Mf'g Co.
- M.C. Lynn   - M.C. Lynn
- J. Fredericks Company   - G. Fredericks Company
- Wandermann, B.S.   - Wanderman, B.S.

14.____

LIST 15
- 4283910293   - 4283010203
- 992018273648   - 992018273848
- 620   - 629
- 752937273   - 752937373
- 5392   - 5392

15.____

LIST 16
- Waldorf Hotel   - Waldorf Hotel
- Aaron Machinery Co.   - Aaron Machinery Co.
- Caroline Ann Locke   - Caroline Ane Locke
- McCabe Mfg. Co.   - McCabe Mfg. Co.
- R.L. Landres   - R.L. Landers

16.____

LIST 17
- 68391028364   - 68391028394
- 68293   - 68293
- 739201   - 739201
- 72839201   - 72839211
- 739917   - 739719

17.____

LIST 18
- Balsam M.M.   - Balsamm, M.M.
- Steinway & Co.   - Stienway & M. Co.
- Eugene Elliott   - Eugene A. Elliott
- Leonard Loan Co.   - Leonard Loan Co.
- Frederick Morgan   - Frederick Morgen

18.____

LIST 19
- 8929   - 9820
- 392836472829   - 392836572829
- 462   - 4622039271
- 827   - 2039276837
- 53829   - 54829

19.____

LIST 20
- Danielson's Hofbrau   - Danielson's Hafbrau
- Edward A. Truarme   - Edward A. Truame
- Insulite Co.   - Insulite Co.
- Reisler Shoe Corp.   - Rielser Shoe Corp.
- L.L. Thompson   - L.L. Thompson

20.____

4 (#2)

LIST 21   21.____
    92839102837   - 92839102837
    58891028   - 58891028
    7291728   - 7291928
    272839102839   - 272839102839
    428192   - 428102

LIST 22   22.____
    K.L. Veiller   - K.L. Veiller
    Webster, Roy   - Webster, Ray
    Drasner Spring Co.   - Drasner Spring Co.
    Edward J. Cravenport   - Edward J. Cravanport
    Harold Field   - Harold A. Field

LIST 23   23.____
    2293   - 2293
    4283910293   - 5382910292
    871928374012   - 871928374912
    68293   - 68393
    8120364927   - 81293649271

LIST 24   24.____
    Tappe, Inc   - Tappe, Inc.
    A.M. Wentingworth   - A.M. Wentinworth
    Scott A. Elliott   - Scott A. Elliott
    Echeverria Corp.   - Echeverria Corp.
    Bradford Victor Company - Bradford Victer Company

LIST 25   25.____
    4820384   - 4820384
    393019283745   - 283919283745
    63917102   - 63927102
    91029354829   - 91029354829
    48291728   - 48291728

5 (#2)
KEY (CORRECT ANSWERS)

1.	1	11.	1
2.	3	12.	3
3.	2	13.	4
4.	2	14.	2
5.	4	15.	1
6.	2	16.	3
7.	3	17.	2
8.	4	18.	1
9.	2	19.	1
10.	3	20.	2

21.	3
22.	2
23.	1
24.	2
25.	4

EXAMINATION SECTION
TEST 1

DIRECTIONS: Each question or incomplete statement is followed by several suggested answers or completions. Select the one that BEST answers the question or completes the statement. *PRINT THE LETTER OF THE CORRECT ANSWER IN THE SPACE AT THE RIGHT.*

1. A supervisor may be required to help train a newly appointed clerk. Which of the following is LEAST important for a newly appointed clerk to know in order to perform his work efficiently?
   A. Acceptable ways of answering and recording telephone calls
   B. The number of files in the storage files unit
   C. The filing methods used by his unit
   D. Proper techniques for handling visitors

   1.____

2. In your agency you have the responsibility of processing clients who have appointments with agency representatives. On a particularly busy day, a client comes to your desk and insists that she must see the person handling her case although she has no appointment.
   Under the circumstances, your FIRST action should be to
   A. show her the full appointment schedule
   B. give her an appointment for another day
   C. ask her to explain the urgency
   D. tell her to return later in the day

   2.____

3. Which of the following practices is BEST for a supervisor to use when assigning work to his staff?
   A. Give workers with seniority the most difficult jobs
   B. Assign all unimportant work to the slower workers
   C. Permit each employee to pick the job he prefers
   D. Make assignments based on the workers' abilities

   3.____

4. In which of the following instances is a supervisor MOST justified in giving commands to people under his supervision? When
   A. they delay in following instructions which have been given to them clearly
   B. they become relaxed and slow about work, and he wants to speed up their production
   C. he must direct them in an emergency situation
   D. he is instructing them on jobs that are unfamiliar to them

   4.____

5. Which of the following supervisory actions or attitudes is MOST likely to result in getting subordinates to try to do as much work as possible for a supervisor? He
   A. shows that his most important interest is in schedules and production goals
   B. consistently pressures his staff to get the work out

   5.____

C. never fails to let them know he is in charge
D. considers their abilities and needs while requiring that production goals be met

6. Assume that a supervisor has been explaining certain regulations to a new clerk under his supervision.
The MOST efficient way for the supervisor to make sure that the clerk has understood the explanation is to
   A. give him written materials on the regulations
   B. ask him if he has any further questions about the regulations
   C. ask him specific questions based on what has just been explained to him
   D. watch the way he handles a situation involving these regulations

6._____

7. One of your unit clerks has been assigned to work for a Mr. Jones in another office for several days. At the end of the first day, Mr. Jones, saying the clerk was not satisfactory, asks that she not be assigned to him again. This clerk is one of your most dependable workers, and no previous complaints about her work have come to you from any other outside assignments.
To get to the root of this situation, your FIRST action should be to
   A. ask Mr. Jones to explain in what way her work was unsatisfactory
   B. ask the clerk what she did that Mr. Jones considered unsatisfactory
   C. check with supervisors for whom she previously worked to see if your own rating of her is in error
   D. tell Mr. Jones to pick the clerk he would prefer to have work for him the next time

7._____

8. A senior typist, still on probation, is instructed to type, as quickly as possible, one section of a draft of a long, complex report. Her part must be typed and readable before another part of the report can be written. Asked when she can have the report ready, she gives her supervisor an estimate of a day longer than she knows it will actually take. She then finishes the job a day sooner than the date given her supervisor.
The judgment shown by the senior typist in giving an overestimate of time in a situation like this is, in general,
   A. *good*, because it prevents the supervisor from thinking she works slowly
   B. *good*, because it keeps unrealistic supervisors from expecting too much
   C. *bad*, because she should have used the time left to further check and proofread her work
   D. *bad*, because schedules and plans for other parts of the project may have been based on her false estimate

8._____

9. Suppose a new clerk, still on probation, is placed under your supervision and refuses to do a job you ask him to do.
What is the FIRST thing you should do?
   A. Explain that you are the supervisor and he must follow your instructions
   B. Tell him he may be suspended if he refuses
   C. Ask someone else to do the job and rate him accordingly
   D. Ask for his reason for objecting to the request

9._____

10. As a supervisor of a small group of people, you have blamed worker A for something that you later find out was really done by worker B.
    The BEST thing for you to do now would be to
    A. say nothing to worker A but criticize worker B for his mistake while worker A is near so that A will realize that you know who made the mistake
    B. speak to each worker separately, apologize to worker A for your mistake, and discuss worker B's mistake with him
    C. bring both workers together, apologize to worker A for your mistake, and discuss worker B's mistake with him
    D. say nothing now but be careful about mixing up worker A with worker B in the future

10.____

11. You have just learned one of your staff is grumbling that she thinks you are not pleased with her work. As far as you're concerned, this isn't true at all. In fact, you've paid no particular attention to this worker lately because you've been very busy. You have just finished preparing an important report and *breaking in* a new clerk.
    Under the circumstances, the BEST thing to do is
    A. ignore her; after all, it's just a figment of her imagination
    B. discuss the matter with her now to try to find out and eliminate the cause of this problem
    C. tell her not to worry about it; you haven't had time to think about her work
    D. make a note to meet with her at a later date in order to straighten out the situation

11.____

12. A most important job of a supervisor is to positively motivate employees to increase their work production.
    Which of the following LEAST indicates that a group of workers has been positively motivated?
    A. Their work output becomes constant and stable.
    B. Their cooperation at work becomes greater.
    C. They begin to show pride in the product of their work.
    D. They show increased interest in their work

12.____

13. Which of the following traits would be LEAST important in considering a person for a merit increase?
    A. Punctuality
    B. Using initiative successfully
    C. High rate of production
    D. Resourcefulness

13.____

14. Of the following, the action LEAST likely to gain a supervisor the cooperation of his staff is for him to
    A. give each person consideration as an individual
    B. be as objective as possible when evaluating work performance
    C. rotate the least popular assignments
    D. expect subordinates to be equally competent

14.____

15. It has been said that, for the supervisor, nothing can beat the *face-to-face* communication of talking to one subordinate at a time.
    This method is, however, LEAST appropriate to use when
    A. supervisor is explaining a change in general office procedure
    B. subject is of personal importance
    C. supervisor is conducting a yearly performance evaluation of all employees
    D. supervisor must talk to some of his employees concerning their poor attendance and punctuality

15.____

16. While you are on the telephone answering a question about your agency, a visitor comes to your desk and starts to ask you a question. There is no emergency or urgency in either situation, that of the phone call or that of answering the visitor's question.
    In this case, you should
    A. continue to answer the person on the telephone until you are finished and then tell the visitor you are sorry to have kept him waiting
    B. excuse yourself to the person on the telephone and tell the visitor that you will be with him as soon as you have finished on the phone
    C. explain to the person on the telephone that you have a visitor and must shorten the conversation
    D. continue to answer the person on the phone while looking up occasionally at the visitor to let him know that you know he is waiting

16.____

17. While speaking on the telephone to someone who called, you are disconnected.
    The FIRST thing you should do is
    A. hang up but try to keep your line free to receive the call back
    B. immediately get the dial tone and continually dial the person who called you until you reach him
    C. signal the switchboard operator and ask her to re-establish the connection
    D. dial O for Operator and explain that you were disconnected

17.____

18. The type of speech used by an office worker in telephone conversations greatly affects the communicator.
    Of the following, the BEST way to express your ideas when telephoning is with a vocabulary that consists mainly of _____ words.
    A. formal, intellectual sounding   B. often used colloquial
    C. technical, emphatic   D. simple, descriptive

18.____

19. Suppose a clerk under your supervision has taken a personal phone call and is at the same time needed to answer a question regarding an assignment being handled by another member of your office. He appears confused as to what he should do. How should you instruct him later as to how to handle a similar situation?
    You should tell him to
    A. tell the caller to hold on while he answers the question
    B. tell the caller to call back a little later

19.____

C. return the call during an assigned break
D. finish the conversation quickly and answer the question

20. You are asked to place a telephone call by your supervisor. When you place the call, you receive what appears to be a wrong number.
Of the following, you should FIRST
    A. check the number with your supervisor to see if the number he gave you is correct
    B. ask the person on the other end what his number is and who he is
    C. check with the person on the other end to see if the number you dialed is the number you received
    D. apologize to the person on the other end for disturbing him and hang up

20._____

Questions 21-30.

DIRECTIONS: WORD MEANING
Each of Questions 21 through 30 contains a word in capitals followed by four suggested meanings of the word. For each question, choose the BEST meaning and write the letter of the best meaning in the space at the right.

21. ACCURATE
    A. correct   B. useful   C. afraid   D. careless

21._____

22. ALTER
    A. copy   B. change   C. repeat   D. agree

22._____

23. DOCUMENT
    A. outline   B. agreement   C. blueprint   D. record

23._____

24. INDICATE
    A. listen   B. show   C. guess   D. try

24._____

25. INVENTORY
    A. custom   B. discovery   C. warning   D. list

25._____

26. ISSUE
    A. annoy   B. use up   C. give out   D. gain

26._____

27. NOTIFY
    A. inform   B. promise   C. approve   D. strength

27._____

28. ROUTINE
    A. path   B. mistake   C. habit   D. journey

28._____

29. TERMINATE
    A. rest   B. start   C. deny   D. end

29._____

30. TRANSMIT
    A. put in   B. send   C. stop   D. go across

30._____

Questions 31-35.

DIRECTIONS: READING COMPREHENSION
Questions 31 through 35 test how well you understand what you read. It will be necessary for you to read carefully because your answers to these questions should be based SOLELY on the information given in the following paragraphs.

The recipient gains an impression of a typewritten letter before he begins to read the message. Factors which provide for a good first impression include margins and spacing that are visually pleasing, formal parts of the letter which are correctly placed according to the style of the letter, copy which is free of obvious erasures and over-strikes, and transcript that is even and clear. The problem for the typist is that of how to produce that first, positive impression of her work.

There are several general rules which a typist can follow when she wishes to prepare a properly spaced letter on a sheet of letterhead. Ordinarily, the width of a letter should not be less than four inches nor more than six inches. The side margins should also have a desirable relation to the bottom margin and the space between the letterhead and the body of the letter. Usually the most appealing arrangement is when the side margins are even and the bottom margin is slightly wider than the side margins. In some offices, however, standard line length is used for all business letters, and the secretary then varies the spacing between the date line and the inside address according to the length of the letter.

31. The BEST title for the above paragraphs would be
    A. Writing Office Letters
    B. Making Good First Impressions
    C. Judging Well-Typed Letters
    D. Good Placing and Spacing for Office Letters

32. According to the above paragraphs, which of the following might be considered the way in which people very quickly judge the quality of work which has been typed?
    By
    A. measuring the margins to see if they are correct
    B. looking at the spacing and cleanliness of the typescript
    C. scanning the body of the letter for meaning
    D. reading the date line and address for errors

33. What, according to the above paragraphs, would be definitely UNDESIRABLE as the average line length of a typed letter?
    A. 4"   B. 5"   C. 6"   D. 7"

34. According to the above paragraphs, when the line length is kept standard, the secretary
    A. does not have to vary the spacing at all since this also is standard
    B. adjusts the spacing between the date line and inside address for different lengths of letters
    C. uses the longest line as a guideline for spacing between the date line and inside address
    D. varies the number of spaces between the lines

35. According to the above paragraphs, side margins are MOST pleasing when they   35._____
    A. are even and somewhat smaller than the bottom margin
    B. are slightly wider than the bottom margin
    C. vary with the length of the letter
    D. are figured independently from the letterhead and the body of the letter

Questions 36-40.

DIRECTIONS: CODING

    Name of Applicant   H A N G S B R U K E
    Test Code   c o m p l e x i t y
    File Number   0 1 2 3 4 5 6 7 8 9

Assume that each of the above capital letters is the first letter of the name of an applicant, that the small letter directly beneath each capital letter is the test code for the applicant, and that the number directly beneath each code letter is the file number for the applicant.

In each of the following Questions 36 through 40, the test code letters and the file numbers in Columns 2 and 3 should correspond to the capital letters in Column 1. For each question, look at each column carefully and mark your answer as follows:
    If there is an error only in Column 2, mark your answer A.
    If there is an error only in Column 3, mark your answer B.
    If there is an error in both Columns 2 and 3, mark your answer C.
    If both Columns 2 and 3 are correct, mark your answer D.

The following sample question is given to help you understand the procedure.

SAMPLE QUESTION

Column 1	Column 2	Column 3
AKEHN	otyci	18902

In Column 2, the final test code letter *i* should be *m*. Column 3 is correctly coded in Column 1. Since there is an error only in Column 2, the answer is A.

	Column 1	Column 2	Column 3	
36.	NEKKU	mytti	29987	36._____
37.	KRAEB	txlye	86095	37._____
38.	ENAUK	ymoit	92178	38._____
39.	REANA	xeomo	69121	39._____
40.	EKHSE	ytcxy	97049	

Questions 41-50.

DIRECTIONS: ARITHMETICAL REASONING
Solve the following problems.

41. If a secretary answered 28 phone calls and typed the addresses for 112 credit statements in one morning, what is the RATIO of phone calls answered to credit statements typed for that period of time?
   A. 1:4   B. 1:7   C. 2:3   D. 3:5

42. According to a suggested filing system, no more than 10 folders should be filed behind any one file guide, and from 15 to 25 file guides should be used in each file drawer for easy finding and filing.
   The MAXIMUM number of folders that a five-drawer file cabinet can hold to allow easy finding and filing is
   A. 550   B. 750   C. 1,100   D. 1,250

43. An employee had a starting salary of $32,902. He received a salary increase at the end of each year, and at the end of the seventh year, his salary was $36,738.
   What was his AVERAGE annual increase in salary over these seven years?
   A. $510   B. $538   C. $548   D. $572

44. The 55 typists and 28 senior clerks in a certain agency were paid a total of $1,943,200 in salaries for the year.
   If the average annual salary of a typist was $22,400, the average annual salary of a senior clerk was
   A. $25,400   B. $26,600   C. $26,800   D. $27,000

45. A typist has been given a three-page report to type. She has finished typing the first two pages. The first page has 283 words, and the second page has 366 words.
   If the total report consists of 954 words, how many words will she have to type on the third page of the report?
   A. 202   B. 287   C. 305   D. 313

46. In one day, Clerk A processed 30% more forms than Clerk B, and Clerk C processed 11/4 as many forms as Clerk A.
   If Clerk B processed 40 forms, how many MORE forms were processed by Clerk C?
   A. 12   B. 13   C. 21   D. 25

47. A clerk who earns a gross salary of $452 every week has the following deductions taken from her paycheck: 17½% for City, State, Federal taxes, and for Social Security, $1.20 for health insurance, and $6.10 for union dues.
   The amount of her take-home pay is
   A. $286.40   B. $312.40   C. $331.60   D. $365.60

48. In 2022 an agency spent $400 to buy pencils at a cost of $1 a dozen. If the agency used ¾ of these pencils in 2022 and used the same number of pencils in 2023, how many MORE pencils did it have to buy to have enough pencils for all of 2023?

   A. 1,200   B. 2,400   C. 3,600   D. 4,800

49. A clerk who worked in Agency X earned the following salaries: $30,070 the first year, $30,500 the second year, and $30,960 the third year. Another clerk who worked in Agency Y for three years earned $30,550 a year for two years and $30,724 the third year.
The DIFFERENCE between the average salaries received by both clerks over a three-year period is

   A. $98   B. $102   C. $174   D. $282

50. An employee who works over 40 hours in any week receives overtime payment for the extra hours at time and one-half (1½ times) his hourly rate of pay. An employee who earns $15.60 an hour works a total of 45 hours during a certain week.
His TOTAL pay for that week would be

   A. $624.00   B. $702.00   C. $741.00   D. $824.00

KEY (CORRECT ANSWERS)

1. B	11. B	21. A	31. D	41. A
2. C	12. A	22. B	32. B	42. D
3. D	13. A	23. D	33. D	43. C
4. C	14. D	24. B	34. B	44. A
5. D	15. A	25. D	35. A	45. C
6. C	16. B	26. C	36. B	46. D
7. A	17. A	27. A	37. C	47. D
8. D	18. D	28. C	38. D	48. B
9. D	19. C	29. D	39. A	49. A
10. B	20. C	30. B	40. C	50. C

TEST 2

DIRECTIONS: Each question or incomplete statement is followed by several suggested answers or completions. Select the one that BEST answers the question or completes the statement. *PRINT THE LETTER OF THE CORRECT ANSWER IN THE SPACE AT THE RIGHT.*

1. To tell a newly employed clerk to fill a top drawer of a four-drawer cabinet with heavy folders which will be often used and to keep lower drawers only partly filled is
   A. *good*, because a tall person would have to bend unnecessarily if he had to use a lower drawer
   B. *bad*, because the file cabinet may tip over when the top drawer is opened
   C. *good*, because it is the most easily reachable drawer for the average person
   D. *bad*, because a person bending down at another drawer may accidentally bang his head on the bottom of the drawer when he straightens up

2. If you have requisitioned a ream of paper in order to duplicate a single page office announcement, how many announcements can be printed from the one package of paper?
   A. 200   B. 500   C. 700   D. 1,000

3. In the operations of a government agency, a voucher is ORDINARILY used to
   A. refer someone to the agency for a position or assignment
   B. certify that an agency's records of financial transactions are accurate
   C. order payment from agency funds of a stated amount to an individual
   D. enter a statement of official opinion in the records of the agency

4. Of the following types of cards used in filing systems, the one which is generally MOST helpful in locating records which might be filed under more than one subject is the _____ card.
   A. cut
   B. tickler
   C. cross-reference
   D. visible index

5. The type of filing system in which one does NOT need to refer to a card index in order to find the folder is called
   A. alphabetic   B. geographic   C. subject   D. locational

6. Of the following, records management is LEAST concerned with
   A. the development of the best method for retrieving important information
   B. deciding what records should be kept
   C. deciding the number of appointments a client will need
   D. determining the types of folders to be used

7. If records are continually removed from a set of files without *charging* them to the borrower, the filing system will soon become ineffective.
   Of the following terms, the one which is NOT applied to a form used in a charge-out system is a
   A. requisition card
   B. out-folder
   C. record retrieval form
   D. substitution card

8. A new clerk has been told to put 500 cards in alphabetical order. Another clerk suggests that she divide the cards into four groups such as A to F, G to L, M to R, and S to Z, and then alphabetize these four smaller groups.
   The suggested method is
   A. *poor*, because the clerk will have to handle the sheets more than once and will waste time
   B. *good*, because it saves time, is more accurate, and is less tiring
   C. *good*, because she will not have to concentrate on it so much when it is in smaller groups
   D. *bad*, because this method is much more tiring than straight alphabetizing

9. The term that describes the equipment attached to an office computer is
   A. interface   B. network   C. hardware   D. software

10. Suppose a clerk has been given pads of pre-printed forms to use when taking phone messages for others in her office. The clerk is then observed using scraps of paper and not the forms for writing her messages.
    It should be explained that the BEST reason for using the forms is that
    A. they act as a checklist to make sure that the important information is taken
    B. she is expected to do her work in the same way as others in the office
    C. they make sure that unassigned paper is not wasted on phone messages
    D. learning to use these forms will help train her to use more difficult forms

11. Of the following, the one which is spelled INCORRECTLY is
    A. alphabetization
    B. reccommendation
    C. redaction
    D. synergy

12. Of the following, the MAIN reason a stock clerk keeps a perpetual inventory of supplies in the storeroom is that such an inventory will
    A. eliminate the need for a physical inventory
    B. provide a continuous record of supplies on hand
    C. indicate whether a shipment of supplies is satisfactory
    D. dictate the terms of the purchase order

13. As a supervisor, you may be required to handle different types of correspondence.
    Of the following types of letters, it would be MOST important to promptly seal which kind of letters?

A. One marked *confidential*
B. Those containing enclosures
C. Any letter to be sent airmail
D. Those in which carbons will be sent along with the original

14. While opening incoming mail, you notice that one letter indicates that an enclosure was to be included but, even after careful inspection,, you are not able to find the information to which this refers.
Of the following, the thing that you should do FIRST is
    A. replace the letter in its envelope and return it to the sender
    B. file the letter until the sender's office mails the missing information
    C. type out a letter to the sender informing them of their error
    D. make a notation in the margin of the letter that the enclosure was omitted

14._____

15. You have been given a checklist and assigned the responsibility of inspecting certain equipment in the various offices of your agency.
Which of the following is the GREATEST advantage of the checklist?
    A. It indicates which equipment is in greatest demand.
    B. Each piece of equipment on the checklist will be checked only once.
    C. It helps to insure that the equipment listed will not be overlooked.
    D. The equipment listed suggests other equipment you should look for.

15._____

16. Your supervisor has asked you to locate a telephone number for an attorney named Jones, whose office is located at 311 Broadway and whose name is not already listed in your files.
The BEST method for finding the number would be for you to
    A. call the information operator and have her get it for you
    B. look in the alphabetical directory (white pages) under the name Jones at 311 Broadway
    C. refer to the heading Attorney in the yellow pages for the name Jones at 311 Broadway
    D. ask your supervisor who referred her to Mr. Jones, then call that person for the number

16._____

17. An example of material that should NOT be sent by first class mail is a
    A. carbon copy of a letter   B. postcard
    C. business reply card   D. large catalogue

17._____

18. Which of the following BEST describes *office work simplification*?
    A. An attempt to increase the rate of production by speeding up the movements of employees
    B. Eliminating wasteful steps in order to increase efficiency
    C. Making jobs as easy as possible for employees so they will not be overworked
    D. Eliminating all difficult tasks from an office and leaving only simple ones

18._____

19. The duties of a supervisor who is assigned the job of timekeeper may include all of the following EXCEPT 19.____
    A. computing and recording regular hours worked each day in accordance with the normal work schedule
    B. approving requests for vacation leave, sick leave, and annual leave
    C. computing and recording overtime hours worked beyond the normal schedule
    D. determining the total regular hours and total extra hours worked during the week

20. Suppose a clerk under your supervision accidentally opens a personal letter while handling office mail. 20.____
    Under such circumstances, you should tell the clerk to put the letter back in the envelope and
    A. take the letter to the person to whom it belongs and make sure he understands that the clerk did not read it
    B. try to seal the envelope so it won't appear to have been opened
    C. write on the envelope *Sorry, opened by mistake*, and put his initials on it
    D. write on the envelope *Sorry, opened by mistake*, but not put his initials on it

Questions 21-25.

DIRECTIONS: SPELLING
Each Question 21 through 25 consists of three words. In each question, one of the words may be spelled incorrectly or all three may be spelled correctly. For each question, if one of the words is spelled incorrectly, write the letter of the incorrect word in the space at the right. If all three words are spelled correctly, write the letter D in the space at the right.

SAMPLE I: (A) guide   (B) departmint   (C) stranger
SAMPLE II: (A) comply   (B) valuable   (C) window

In Sample Question I, *departmint* is incorrect. It should be spelled *department*. Therefore, B is the answer to Sample Question 1.
In Sample Question II, all three words are spelled correctly. Therefore D is the answer to Sample Question II.

21. A. argument   B. reciept   C. complain   21.____
22. A. sufficient   B. postpone   C. visible   22.____
23. A. expirience   B. dissatisfy   C. alternate   23.____
24. A. occurred   B. noticable   C. appendix   24.____
25. A. anxious   B. guarantee   C. calender   25.____

Questions 26-30.

DIRECTIONS: ENGLISH USAGE
Each Question 26 through 30 contains a sentence. Read each sentence carefully to decide whether it is correct. Then, in the space at the right, mark your answer:
A. if the sentence is incorrect because of bad grammar or sentence structure
B. of the sentence is incorrect because of bad punctuation
C. if the sentence is incorrect because of bad capitalization
D. if the sentence is correct

Each incorrect sentence has only one type of error. Consider a sentence correct if it has no errors, although there may be other correct ways of saying the same thing.

SAMPLE QUESTION I: One of our clerks were promoted yesterday.
The subject of this sentence is *one*, so the verb should be *was promoted* instead of *were promoted*. Since the sentence is incorrect because of bad grammar, the answer to Sample Question I is A.

SAMPLE QUESTION II: Between you and me, I would prefer not going there.
Since this sentence is correct, the answer to Sample Question II is D.

26. The National alliance of Businessmen is trying to persuade private businesses to hire youth in the summertime. 26.____

27. The supervisor who is on vacation, is in charge of processing vouchers. 27.____

28. The activity of the committee at its conferences is always stimulating. 28.____

29. After checking the addresses again, the letters went to the mailroom. 29.____

30. The director, as well as the employees, are interested in sharing the dividends. 30.____

Questions 31-40.

DIRECTIONS: FILING
Each Question 31 through 40 contains four names. For each question, choose the name that should be FIRST if the four names are to be arranged in alphabetical order in accordance with the Rules for Alphabetical Filing given below. Read these rules carefully. Then, for each question, indicate in the correspondingly numbered space at the right the letter before the name that should be FIRST in alphabetical order.

RULES FOR ALPHABETICAL FILING

Names of People

1. The names of people are filed in strict alphabetical order, first according to the last name, then according to first name or initial, and finally according to middle name or initial. For example: George Allen comes before Edward Bell, and Leonard P. Reston comes before Lucille B. Reston.

2. When last names are the same, for example A. Green and Agnes Green, the one with the initial comes before the one with the name written out when the first initials are identical.

3. When first and last names are alike and the middle initial is given, for example John David Doe and John Devoe Doe, the names should be filed in the alphabetical order of the middle names.

4. When first and last names are the same, a name without a middle initial comes before one with a middle name or initial. For example, John Doe comes before both John A. Doe and John Alan Doe.

5. When first and last names are the same, a name with a middle initial comes before one with a middle name beginning with the same initial. For example: Jack R. Herts comes before Jack Richard Hertz.

6. Prefixes such as De, O', Mac, Mc, and Van are filed as written and are treated as part of the names to which they are connected. For example: Robert O'Dea is filed before David Olsen.

7. Abbreviated names are treated as if they were spelled out. For example: Chas. is filed as Charles and Thos. is filed as Thomas.

8. Titles and designations such as Dr., Mr., and Prof. are disregarded in filing.

Names of Organizations

1. The names of business organizations are filed according to the order in which each word in the name appears. When an organization name bears the name of a person, it is filed according to the rules for filing names of people as given above. For example, William Smith Service Co. comes before Television Distributors, Inc.

2. Where bureau, board, office or department appears as the first part of the title of a governmental agency, that agency should be filed under the word in the title expressing the chief function of the agency. For example: Bureau of the Budget would be filed as if written Budget, (Bureau of the). The Department of Personnel would be filed as if written Personnel (Department of).

3. When the following words are part of an organization, they are disregarded: the, of, and.

4. When there are numbers in a name, they are treated as if they were spelled out. For example: 10th Street Bootery is filed as Tenth Street Bootery.

   SAMPLE QUESTION: A. Jane Earl   (2)
                      B. James A. Earle   (4)
                      C. James Earl   (1)
                      D. J. Earle   (3)

   The numbers in parentheses show the proper alphabetical order in which these names should be filed. Since the name that should be filed FIRST is James Earl, the answer to the sample question is C.

31. A. Majorca Leather Goods   B. Robert Majorca and Sons   31.____
    C. Maintenance Management Corp.   D. Majestic Carpet Mills

32. A. Municipal Telephone Service   B. Municipal Reference Library   32.____
    C. Municipal Credit Union   D. Municipal Broadcasting System

33. A. Robert B. Pierce   B. R. Bruce Pierce   33.____
    C. Ronald Pierce   D. Robert Bruce Pierce

34. A. Four Seasons Sports Club   B. 14 Street Shopping Center   34.____
    C. Forty Thieves Restaurant   D. 42nd St. Theaters

35. A. Franco Franceschini   B. Amos Franchini   35.____
    C. Sandra Franceschia   D. Lilie Franchinesca

36. A. Chas. A. Levine   B. Kurt Levene   36.____
    C. Charles Levine   D. Kurt E. Levene

37. A. Prof. Geo. Kinkaid   B. Mr. Alan Kinkaid   37.____
    C. Dr. Albert A. Kinkade   D. Kincade Liquors Inc.

38. A. Department of Public Events   B. Office of the Public Administrator   38.____
    C. Queensborough Public Library   D. Department of Public Health

39. A. Martin Luther King, Jr. Towers B. Metro North Plaza   39.____
    C. Manhattanville Houses   D. Marble Hill Houses

40. A. Dr. Arthur Davids   B. The David Check Cashing Service   40.____
    C. A.C. Davidsen   D. Milton Davidoff

Questions 41-45.

DIRECTIONS: READING COMPREHENSION
Questions 41 through 45 test how well you understand what you read. It will be necessary for you to read carefully because your answers to these questions should be based SOLELY on the information given in the following paragraph.

Work standards presuppose an ability to measure work. Measurement in office management is needed for several reasons. First, it is necessary to evaluate the overall efficiency of the office itself. It is then essential to measure the efficiency of each particular section or unit and that of the individual worker. To plan and control the work of sections and units, one must have measurement. A program of measurement goes hand in hand with a program of standards. One can have measurement without standards, but one cannot have work standards without measurement. Providing data on amount of work done and time expended, measurement does not deal with the amount of energy expended by an individual although in many cases such energy may be in direct proportion to work output. Usually from two-thirds to three fourths of all work can be measured. However, less than two-thirds of all work is actually measured because measurement difficulties are encountered when office work is non-repetitive and irregular, or when it is primarily mental rather than manual. These obstacles are often used as excuses for non-measurement far more frequently than is justified.

41. According to the paragraph, an office manager cannot set work standards unless he can
    A. plan the amount of work to be done
    B. control the amount of work that is done
    C. estimate accurately the quantity of work done
    D. delegate the amount of work to be done to efficient workers

42. According to the paragraph, the type of office work that would be MOST difficult to measure would be
    A. checking warrants for accuracy of information
    B. recording payroll changes
    C. processing applications
    D. making up a new system of giving out supplies

43. According to the paragraph, the actual amount of work that is measured is _____ of all work.
    A. less than two-thirds
    B. two-thirds to three-fourths
    C. less than three-sixths
    D. more than three-fourths

44. Which of the following would be MOST difficult to determine by using measurement techniques?
    A. The amount of work that is accomplished during a certain period of time
    B. The amount of work that should be planned for a period of time
    C. How much time is needed to do a certain task
    D. The amount of incentive a person must have to do his job

45. The one of the following which is the MOST suitable title for the paragraph is:
    A. How Measurement of Office Efficiency Depends on Work Standards
    B. Using Measurement for Office Management and Efficiency
    C. Work Standards and the Efficiency of the Office Worker
    D. Managing the Office Using Measured Work Standards

Questions 46-50.

DIRECTIONS: **INTERPRETING STATISTICAL DATA**
Questions 46 through 50 are to be answered using the information given in the following table.

AGE COMPOSITION IN THE LABOR FORCE IN CITY A
(2010-2020)

	Age Group	2010	2015	2020
Men	14-24	8,430	10,900	14,340
	25-44	22,200	22,350	26,065
	45+	17,550	19,800	21,970
Women	14-24	4,450	6,915	7,680
	25-44	9,080	10,010	11,550
	45+	7,325	9,470	13,180

46. The GREATEST increase in the number of people in the labor force between 2010 and 2015 occurred among
    A. men between the ages of 14 and 24
    B. men age 45 and over
    C. women between the ages of 14 and 24
    D. women age 45 and over

46.____

47. If the total number of women of all ages in the labor force increases from 2020 to 2025 by the same number as it did from 2015 to 2020, the TOTAL number of women of all ages in the labor force in 2025 will be
    A. 27,425   B. 29,675   C. 37,525   D. 38,425

47.____

48. The total increase in number of women in the labor force from 2010 to 2015 differs from the total increase of men in the same years by being _____ than that of men.
    A. 770 less   B. 670 more   C. 770 more   D. 1,670 more

48.____

49. In the year 2010, the proportion of married women in each group was as follows: 1/5 of the women in the 14-24 age group, 1/4 of those in the 25-44 age group, and 2/5 of those 45 and over.
How many married women were in the labor force in 2010?
    A. 4,625   B. 5,990   C. 6,090   D. 7,910

49.____

50. The 14-24 age group of men in the labor force from 2010 to 2020 increased by APPROXIMATELY
    A. 40%   B. 65%   C. 70%   D. 75%

50.____

KEY (CORRECT ANSWERS)

1. B	11. B	21. B	31. C	41. C
2. B	12. B	22. D	32. D	42. D
3. C	13. A	23. A	33. B	43. A
4. C	14. D	24. B	34. D	44. D
5. A	15. C	25. C	35. C	45. B
6. C	16. C	26. C	36. B	46. A
7. C	17. D	27. B	37. D	47. D
8. B	18. B	28. D	38. B	48. B
9. C	19. B	29. A	39. A	49. C
10. A	20. C	30. A	40. B	50. C

EXAMINATION SECTION
TEST 1

DIRECTIONS: Each question or incomplete statement is followed by several suggested answers or completions. Select the one that BEST answers the question or completes the statement. *PRINT THE LETTER OF THE CORRECT ANSWER IN THE SPACE AT THE RIGHT.*

1. Suppose that you are requested to transmit to the stenographers in your bureau an order curtailing certain privileges that they have been enjoying. You anticipate that your staff may resent curtailment of such privileges. Of the following, the BEST action for you to take is to

    A. impress upon your staff that an order is an order and must be obeyed
    B. attempt to explain to your staff the probable reasons for curtailing their privileges
    C. excuse the curtailment of privileges by saying that the welfare of the staff was evidently not considered
    D. warn your staff that violation of an order may be considered sufficient cause for immediate dismissal

1.____

2. The supervisor should set a good example.
   Of the following, the CHIEF implication of the above statement is that the supervisor should

    A. behave as he expects his workers to behave
    B. know as much about the work as his workers do
    C. keep his workers informed of what he is doing
    D. keep ahead of his workers

2.____

3. Of the following, the LEAST desirable procedure for the competent supervisor to follow is to

    A. organize his work before taking responsibility for helping others with theirs
    B. avoid schedules and routines when he is busy
    C. be flexible in planning and carrying out his responsibilities
    D. secure the support of his staff in organizing the total job of the unit

3.____

4. Evaluation helps the worker by increasing his security.
   Of the following, the BEST justification for this statement is that

    A. security and growth depend upon knowledge by the worker of the agency's evaluation
    B. knowledge of his evaluation by agency and supervisor will stimulate the worker to better performance
    C. evaluation enables the supervisor and worker to determine the reasons for the worker's strengths and weaknesses
    D. the supervisor and worker together can usually recognize and deal with any worker's insecurity

4.____

5. A supervisor may encourage his subordinates to make suggestions by

    A. keeping a record of the number of suggestions an employee makes
    B. providing a suggestion box

5.____

99

C. outlining a list of possible suggestions
D. giving credit to a subordinate whose suggestion has been accepted and used

6. If you were required to give service ratings to employees under your supervision, you should consider as MOST important during the current period the

A. personal characteristics and salary and grade of an employee
B. length of service and the volume of work performed
C. previous service rating given him
D. personal characteristics and the quality of work of an employee

7. A supervisor must consider many factors in evaluating a worker whom he has supervised for a considerable time. In evaluating the capacity of such a worker to use independent judgment, the one of the following to which the supervisor should generally give MOST consideration is the worker's

A. capacity to establish good relationships with people (clients and colleagues)
B. educational background
C. emotional stability
D. the quality and judgment shown by the investigator in previous work situations known to the supervisor

8. Experts in the field of personnel relations feel that it is generally a bad practice for subordinate employees to become aware of pending or contemplated changes in policy or organizational set-up via the "grapevine" CHIEFLY because

A. evidence that one or more responsible officials have proved untrustworthy will undermine confidence in the agency
B. the information disseminated by this method is seldom entirely accurate and generally spreads needless unrest among the subordinate staff
C. the subordinate staff may conclude that the administration feels the staff cannot be trusted with the true information
D. the subordinate staff may conclude that the administration lacks the courage to make an unpopular announcement through official channels

9. Assume that a supervisor praises his subordinates for satisfactory aspects of their work only when he is about to criticize them for unsatisfactory aspects of their work. Such a practice is UNDESIRABLE primarily because

A. his subordinates may expect to be praised for their work even if it is unsatisfactory
B. praising his subordinates for some aspects of their work while criticizing other aspects will weaken the effects of the criticisms
C. his subordinates would be more receptive to criticism if it were followed by praise
D. his subordinates may come to disregard praise and wait for criticism to be given

10. The one of the following which would be the BEST reason for an agency to eliminate a procedure for obtaining and recording certain information is that

A. it is no longer legally required to obtain the information
B. there is an advantage in obtaining the information
C. the information could be compiled on the basis of other information available
D. the information obtained is sometimes incorrect

11. In determining the type and number of records to be kept in an agency, it is important to recognize that records are of value PRIMARILY as

    A. raw material to be used in statistical analysis
    B. sources of information about the agency's activities
    C. by-products of the activities carried on by the agency
    D. data for evaluating the effectiveness of the agency

12. Assume that you are a supervisor. One of the workers under your supervision is careless about the routine aspects of his work.
    Of the following, the action MOST likely to develop in this worker a better attitude toward job routines is to demonstrate that

    A. it is just as easy to do his job the right way
    B. organization of his job will leave more time for field work
    C. the routine part of the job is essential to performing a good piece of work
    D. job routines are a responsibility of the worker

13. A supervisor can MOST effectively secure necessary improvement in a worker's office work by

    A. encouraging the worker to keep abreast of his work
    B. relating the routine part of his job to the total job to be done
    C. helping the worker to establish a good system for covering his office work and holding him to it
    D. informing the worker that he will be required to organize his work more efficiently

14. A supervisor should offer criticism in such a manner that the criticism is helpful and not overwhelming.
    Of the following, the LEAST valid inference that can be drawn on the basis of the above statement is that a supervisor should

    A. demonstrate that the criticism is partial and not total
    B. give criticism in such a way that it does not undermine the worker's self-confidence
    C. keep his relationships with the worker objective
    D. keep criticism directed towards general work performance

15. The one of the following areas in which a worker may LEAST reasonably expect direct assistance from the supervisor is in

    A. building up rapport with all clients
    B. gaining insight into the unmet needs of clients
    C. developing an understanding of community resources
    D. interpreting agency policies and procedures

16. You are informed that a worker under your supervision has submitted a letter complaining of unfair service rating. Of the following, the MOST valid assumption for you to make concerning this worker is that he should be

    A. more adequately supervised in the future
    B. called in for a supervisory conference
    C. given a transfer to some other unit where he may be more happy
    D. given no more consideration than any other inefficient worker

17. Assume that you are a supervisor. You find that a somewhat bewildered worker, newly appointed to the department, hesitates to ask questions for fear of showing his ignorance and jeopardizing his position.
    Of the following, the BEST procedure for you to follow is to

    A. try to discover the reason for his evident fear of authority
    B. tell him that when he is in doubt about a procedure or a policy he should consult his fellow workers
    C. develop with the worker a plan for more frequent supervisory conferences
    D. explain why each staff member is eager to give him available information that will help him do a good job

18. In order to teach an employee to develop an objective approach, the BEST action for the supervisor to take is to help the worker to

    A. develop a sincere interest in his job
    B. understand the varied responsibilities that are an integral part of his job
    C. differentiate clearly between himself as a friend and as an employee
    D. find satisfaction in his work

19. Of the following, the MOST effective method of helping a newly appointed employee adjust to his new job is to

    A. assure him that with experience his uncertain attitudes will be replaced by a professional approach
    B. help him, by accepting him as he is, to have confidence in his ability to handle the job
    C. help him to be on guard against the development of punitive attitudes
    D. help him to recognize the mutability of the agency's policies and procedures

20. Suppose that, as a supervisor, you have scheduled an individual conference with an experienced employee under your supervision.
    Of the following, the BEST plan of action for this conference is to

    A. discuss the work that the employee is most interested in
    B. plan with the employee to cover any problems that are difficult for him
    C. advise the employee that the conference is his to do with as he sees fit
    D. spot check the employee's work in advance and select those areas for discussion in which the employee has done poor work

21. Of the following, the CHIEF function of a supervisor should be to

    A. assist in the planning of new policies and the evaluation of existing ones
    B. promote congenial relationships among members of the staff
    C. achieve optimum functioning of each unit and each worker
    D. promote the smooth functioning of job routines

22. The competent supervisor must realize the importance of planning.
    Of the following, the aspect of planning which is LEAST appropriately considered a responsibility of the supervisor is

    A. long-range planning for the proper functioning of his unit
    B. planning to take care of peak and slack periods
    C. planning to cover agency policies in group conferences

D. long-range planning to develop community resources

23. The one of the following objectives which should be of LEAST concern to the supervisor in the performance of his duties is to

    A. help the worker to make friends with all of his fellow employees
    B. be impartial and fair to all members of the staff
    C. stimulate the worker's growth on the job
    D. meet the needs of the individual employee

24. The one of the following which is LEAST properly considered a direct responsibility of the supervisor is

    A. liaison between the staff and the administrator
    B. interpreting administrative orders and procedures to the employee
    C. training new employees
    D. maintaining staff morale at a high level

25. If an employee shows excessive submission which indicates a need for dependence on the supervisor in handling an assignment, it would be MOST advisable for the supervisor to

    A. indicate firmly that the employee-supervisor relationship does not call for submission
    B. define areas of responsibility of employee and of superior
    C. recognize the employee's need to be sustained and supported and help him by making decisions for him
    D. encourage the employee to do his best to overcome his handicap

KEY (CORRECT ANSWERS)

1. B		11. B	
2. A		12. D	
3. B		13. B	
4. C		14. D	
5. D		15. A	
6. D		16. B	
7. D		17. C	
8. B		18. C	
9. D		19. B	
10. C		20. B	

21. C
22. D
23. A
24. A
25. B

TEST 2

DIRECTIONS: Each question or incomplete statement is followed by several suggested answers or completions. Select the one that BEST answers the question or completes the statement. *PRINT THE LETTER OF THE CORRECT ANSWER IN THE SPACE AT THE RIGHT.*

1. Assume that, as a supervisor, you are conducting a group conference.
   Of the following, the BEST procedure for you to follow in order to stimulate group discussion is to

   A. permit the active participation of all members
   B. direct the discussion to an acceptable conclusion
   C. resolve conflicts of opinion among members of the group
   D. present a question for discussion on which the group members have some knowledge or experience

   1.____

2. Suppose that, as a new supervisor, you wish to inform the staff under your supervision of your methods of operation. Of the following, the BEST procedure for you to follow is to

   A. advise the staff that they will learn gradually from experience
   B. inform each employee in an individual conference
   C. call a group conference for this purpose
   D. distribute a written memorandum among all members of the staff

   2.____

3. The MOST constructive and effective method of correcting an employee who has made a mistake is, in general, to

   A. explain that his evaluation is related to his errors
   B. point out immediately where he erred and tell him how it should have been done
   C. show him how to readjust his methods so as to avoid similar errors in the future
   D. try to discover by an indirect method why the error was made

   3.____

4. The MOST effective method for the supervisor to follow in order to obtain the cooperation of an employee under his supervision is, wherever possible, to

   A. maintain a careful record of performance in order to keep the employee on his toes
   B. give the employee recognition in order to promote greater effort and give him more satisfaction in his work
   C. try to gain the employee's cooperation for the good of the service
   D. advise the employee that his advancement on the job depends on his cooperation

   4.____

5. Of the following, the MOST appropriate initial course for an employee to take when he is unable to clarify a policy with his supervisor is to

   A. bring up the problem at the next group conference
   B. discuss the policy immediately with his fellow employees
   C. accept the supervisor's interpretation as final
   D. determine what responsibility he has for putting the policy into effect

   5.____

6. Good administration allows for different treatment of different workers.
   Of the following, the CHIEF implication of this quotation is that

   6.____

A. it would be unfair for the supervisor not to treat all staff members alike
B. fear of favoritism tends to undermine staff morale
C. best results are obtained by individualization within the limits of fair treatment
D. difficult problems call for a different kind of approach

7. The MOST effective and appropriate method of building efficiency and morale in a group of employees is, in general,

   A. by stressing the economic motive
   B. through use of the authority inherent in the position
   C. by a friendly approach to all
   D. by a discipline that is fair but strict

8. Of the following, the LEAST valid basis for the assignment of work to an employee is the

   A. kind of service to be rendered
   B. experience and training of the employee
   C. health and capacity of the employee
   D. racial composition of the community where the office is located

9. The CHIEF justification for staff education, consisting of in-service training, lies in its contribution to

   A. improvement in the quality of work performed
   B. recruitment of a better type of employee
   C. employee morale accruing from a feeling of growth on the job
   D. the satisfaction that the employee gets on his job

10. Suppose that you are a supervisor. An employee no longer with your department requests you, as his former supervisor, to write a letter recommending him for a position with a private organization.
    Of the following, the BEST procedure for you to follow is to include in the letter only information that

    A. will help the applicant get the job
    B. is clear, factual, and substantiated
    C. is known to you personally
    D. can readily be corroborated by personal interview

11. Of the following, the MOST important item on which to base the efficiency evaluation of an employee under your supervision is

    A. the nature of the relationship that he has built up with his fellow employees
    B. how he gets along with his supervisors
    C. his personal habits and skills
    D. the effectiveness of his control over his work

12. According to generally accepted personnel practice, the MOST effective method of building morale in a new employee is to

    A. exercise caution in praising the employee, lest he become overconfident
    B. give sincere and frank commendation whenever possible, in order to stimulate interest and effort

C. praise the employee highly even for mediocre performance so that he will be stimulated to do better
D. warn the employee frequently that he cannot hope to succeed unless he puts forth his best effort

13. Errors made by newly appointed employees often follow a predictable pattern. The one of the following errors likely to have LEAST serious consequences is the tendency of a new employee to

    A. discuss problems that are outside his province with the client
    B. persuade the client to accept the worker's solution of a problem
    C. be too strict in carrying out departmental policy and procedure
    D. depend upon the use of authority due to his inexperience and lack of skill in working with people

14. The MOST effective way for a supervisor to break down a worker's defensive stand against supervisory guidance is to

    A. come to an understanding with him on the mutual responsibilities involved in the job of the employee and supervisor
    B. tell him he must feel free to express his opinions and to discuss basic problems
    C. show him how to develop toward greater objectivity, sensitivity, and understanding
    D. advise him that it is necessary to carry out agency policy and procedures in order to do a good job

15. Of the following, the LEAST essential function of the supervisor who is conducting a group conference should be to

    A. keep attention focused on the purpose of the conference
    B. encourage discussion of controversial points
    C. make certain that all possible viewpoints are discussed
    D. be thoroughly prepared in advance

16. When conducting a group conference, the supervisor should be LEAST concerned with

    A. providing an opportunity for the free interchange of ideas
    B. imparting knowledge and understanding of case work
    C. leading the discussion toward a planned goal
    D. pointing out where individual workers have erred in work practice

17. If the participants in a group conference are unable to agree on the proper application of a concept to the work of a department, the MOST suitable temporary procedure for the supervisor to follow is to

    A. suggest that each member think the subject through before the next meeting
    B. tell the group to examine their differences for possible conflicts with present policies
    C. suggest that practices can be changed because of new conditions
    D. state the acceptable practice in the agency and whether deviations from such practice can be permitted

18. If an employee is to participate constructively in any group discussion, it is MOST important that he have

    A. advance notice of the agenda for the meeting
    B. long experience in the department
    C. knowledge and experience in the particular work
    D. the ability to assume a leadership role

19. Of the following, the MOST important principle for the supervisor to follow when conducting a group discussion is that he should

    A. move the discussion toward acceptance by the group of a particular point of view
    B. express his ideas clearly and succinctly
    C. lead the group to accept the authority inherent in his position
    D. contribute to the discussion from his knowledge and experience

20. The one of the following which is considered LEAST important as a purpose of the group conference is to

    A. provide for a free exchange of ideas among the members of the group
    B. evaluate work methods and procedures in order to protect the members from individual criticism
    C. provide an opportunity to interpret procedures and work practices
    D. pool the experience of the group members for the benefit of all

21. In order for the evaluation conference to stimulate MOST effectively the employee's professional growth on the job, it should

    A. start him thinking, about his present status with the department
    B. show him the necessity for taking stock of his total performance
    C. give him a sense of direction in relation to his future development
    D. give him a better perspective on the work in his department

22. The development of good public relations in the area for which the supervisor is responsible should be considered by the supervisor as

    A. not his responsibility as he is primarily responsible for his employees' services
    B. dependent upon him as he is in the best position to interpret the department to the community
    C. not important to the adequate functioning of the department
    D. a part of his method of carrying out his job responsibility, as what his employees do affect the community

23. Of the following, the MOST valuable and desirable trait in a supervisor is a(n)

    A. ability to get the best work out of his men
    B. ability to inspire his men with the desire to "get ahead in the world"
    C. persuasive manner of speech
    D. tall and commanding appearance

24. The supervisor who is MOST suitable for the general practical needs of a department is the one who gets

   A. a great deal of satisfactory work done although usually handicapped by constant bickering among fellow employees
   B. a great deal of satisfactory work done because of his ability to do a large amount of it himself
   C. less work done than the other supervisors but has unusually high quality work production standards
   D. more than an average amount of satisfactory work done because of the cooperative way in which the employees work for him

25. A supervisor has been transferred to a new section.
    The BEST way for him to get cooperation from his employees would be to

   A. ask the (general manager)(chief) to give him strong support
   B. explain his policy firmly so that the employees cannot blame him for any mistakes made
   C. note the troublemakers and have them transferred out
   D. show his men that he not only is interested in getting work done but also has their welfare in mind

KEY (CORRECT ANSWERS)

1. D
2. C
3. C
4. B
5. D

6. C
7. D
8. D
9. A
10. B

11. D
12. B
13. C
14. A
15. B

16. D
17. D
18. A
19. D
20. B

21. C
22. D
23. A
24. D
25. D

TEST 3

DIRECTIONS: Each question or incomplete statement is followed by several suggested answers or completions. Select the one that BEST answers the question or completes the statement. *PRINT THE LETTER OF THE CORRECT ANSWER IN THE SPACE AT THE RIGHT.*

1. Jones and Smith, who work together, do slightly more than an average amount of work for two men together. But you find that Jones does most of the work while Smith does less than he should.
   To correct this situation, the BEST thing for you as supervisor to do would be to

   A. assign work to Smith for which he must be personally responsible
   B. make a complaint to the bureau chief about Smith but praise Jones
   C. point out to Jones that he does most of the work and that he should urge Smith to do more
   D. require Smith to do more whenever the work of both men together falls below the expected average

1.____

2. You have given a new employee detailed instructions on how he should do a job. When you return a little later, you find that the employee was afraid to start the job because he did not completely understand your instructions.
   In this situation, it would be BEST for you to

   A. assign the man to a job where less intelligence is needed
   B. explain again, illustrating if possible how the job is to be done
   C. explain again and recommend him for dropping at the end of probation if he does not understand
   D. make the man explain why he did not at least start the job

2.____

3. An employee does very good work but has trouble getting to work on time.
   To get him to come on time, the supervisor should

   A. bring him up on charges to stop the lateness once and for all
   B. have him report to the general manager every time he is late
   C. talk over the problem with him to find its cause and possible solution
   D. threaten to transfer him if he cannot get to work early

3.____

4. As supervisor, you observe that an employee keeps making mistakes.
   Of the following, the BEST thing for you to do would be to

   A. make no mention of these mistakes as they gradually disappear with experience
   B. point the mistakes out to the employee in front of the other employees so all may learn from them
   C. talk to the employee privately about these mistakes and show her how to avoid them
   D. try to transfer this employee out in exchange for an employee who can do the work

4.____

5. Proper action by the supervisor could MOST probably prevent work delays in his section caused by

   A. a large number of employees quitting their jobs in the department
   B. the daily assignments of the employees not being properly planned

5.____

C. the inexperience of new employees transferred into his section
D. unexpected delays in processing

6. If, after careful thought, you have definitely decided that one of your employees should be disciplined, it is MOST important for you to realize that

   A. discipline is the best tool for leading workers
   B. discipline should be severe in order to get the best results
   C. the discipline should be delayed so that its full force can be felt
   D. the employee should know why she is being disciplined

7. A knowledge of the experience and abilities of the men working under him is MOST useful to a supervisor in

   A. deciding what type of discipline to exercise when necessary
   B. finding the cause of minor errors in the assignments
   C. making proper work assignments
   D. making vacation schedules

8. A supervisor will be able to train his employees better if he is familiar with basic principles of learning.
   Which one of the following statements about the learning process is MOST correct?

   A. An employee who learns one job quickly will learn any other job quickly.
   B. Emphasizing correct things done by the employee usually gives him an incentive to improve.
   C. Great importance placed on an employee's mistakes is the best way to help him to get rid of them.
   D. It is very hard to teach new methods to middle-aged or older employees.

9. Several experienced employees have resigned. You have decided to arrange for permanent transfers of other experienced employees in your section to fill their jobs, leaving only jobs that new inexperienced employees can fill easily.
   For you, the supervisor, to talk this over with the employees who will be affected by the move would be

   A. *bad;* it would show weakness and wavering by you
   B. *bad;* transfers should be made on the basis of efficiency
   C. *good;* it will help you get better cooperation from the employees involved
   D. *good;* transfers should be made on the basis of seniority

10. An employee under your supervision does much less work than he is capable of.
    What should be your FIRST step in an effort to improve his performance?

    A. Discovering why he is not working up to his full capacity
    B. Going over his mistakes and shortcomings with him to reduce them
    C. Pointing out to him that the quality of his work is below standard
    D. Showing him that the other men produce much more than he does

11. The FIRST thing a supervisor does when he assigns an employee to a new job is to find out what the employee already knows about the job.
    This practice is

A. *good;* mainly because the employees may know more than the supervisor about the job
B. *good;* mainly because this information will help the supervisor in instructing the employee
C. *poor;* mainly because since it is a new job, the employee cannot be expected to know anything
D. *poor;* mainly because the supervisor should first find out how the employee will feel toward the job

12. Your superior has assigned to you a task which, in your opinion, should not be performed at this stage of the operation.
In this situation, it would be BEST for you to

    A. carry out the assignment since your superior is responsible
    B. refuse to carry out the assignment
    C. talk it over with the employees under you to see if they think as you do
    D. talk the matter over with your superior right away

13. It is important for a supervisor to take prompt action upon requests from subordinates MAINLY because

    A. delays in making decisions mean that they must then be made on the basis of facts which can no longer be up-to-date
    B. favorable action on such requests is more likely to result when a decision is made quickly
    C. it is an indication that the supervisor has his work well-organized
    D. promptness in such matters helps maintain good employee morale

14. As a supervisor, you realize that your superior, when under pressure, has a habit of giving you oral orders which are not always clear and also lack sufficient detail. The BEST procedure for you to follow in such situations would be to

    A. obtain clarification by requesting needed details at the time you receive such orders
    B. consider past orders of a similar nature to determine the probable intent of your superior
    C. frequently consult your superior during the course of the job in order to secure the required details to complete the job
    D. request your superior to put all his orders to you in writing

15. Some supervisors have their subordinates meet with them in group discussion of troublesome problems.
The MAIN advantage of such group discussions as a supervisory tool is that they can be directed toward the

    A. appraisal of the personalities involved
    B. development of new policies and regulations
    C. circulation of new material and information
    D. pooling of experience in the solution of common problems

16. The PRINCIPAL disadvantage of using form letters to reply to written complaints made by the public is that such form letters

A. tend to make any investigation of the original complaint rather superficial
B. are limited by their design to handle only a few possible situations that could give rise to complaints
C. lack the desirable element of the personal touch for the recipient
D. tend to lose their effectiveness by quickly becoming obsolete

17. With respect to standard employee grievance procedure, it would be MOST correct to state that

    A. the Commissioner of Labor is the highest ranking official, excepting the judge, who can be involved in a particular grievance
    B. the person with the grievance has the right to be represented by virtually anyone he chooses
    C. the one having the grievance (the grievant) can be represented by the majority organization only if he is a member thereof
    D. time limits are not set concerning adjudication in order to insure the fullest consideration of the particular grievance

18. In order for a supervisor to employ the system of democratic leadership in his supervision, it would generally be BEST for him to

    A. allow his subordinates to assist in deciding on methods of work performance and job assignments but only in those areas where decisions have not been made on higher administrative levels
    B. allow his subordinates to decide how to do the required work, interposing his authority when work is not completed on schedule or is improperly completed
    C. attempt to make assignments of work to individuals only of the type which they enjoy doing
    D. maintain control over the job assignments and work production but allow the subordinates to select methods of work and internal conditions of work at democratically conducted staff conferences

19. In an office in which supervision has been considered quite effective, it has become necessary to press for above-normal production for a limited period to achieve a required goal.
    The one of the following which is a LEAST likely result of this pressure is that

    A. there will be more "gripings" by employees
    B. some workers will do both more and better work than has been normal for them
    C. there will be an enhanced feeling of group unity
    D. there will be increased absenteeism

20. It is the practice of some supervisors, when they believe that it would be desirable for a subordinate to take a particular action in a case, to inform the subordinate of this in the form of a suggestion rather than in the form of a direct order. In general, this method of getting a subordinate to take the desired action is

    A. *inadvisable;* it may create in the mind of the subordinate the impression that the supervisor is uncertain about the efficacy of his plan and is trying to avoid whatever responsibility he may have in resolving the case
    B. *advisable;* it provides the subordinate with the maximum opportunity to use his own judgment in handling the case

C. *inadvisable;* it provides the subordinate with no clear-cut direction and, therefore, is likely to leave him with a feeling of uncertainty and frustration
D. *advisable;* it presents the supervisor's view in a manner which will be most likely to evoke the subordinate's cooperation

21. At a group training conference conducted by a supervisor, one of the employees asks a question which is only partially related to the subject under discussion. He believes that the question was asked to embarrass him since he recently reprimanded the employees for inattention to his work. Under these circumstances, it would generally be BEST for the assistant supervisor to

    A. pointedly ignore the question and the questioner and go on to other matters
    B. request the questioner to remain after the group session, at which time the question and the questioner's attitude will be considered
    C. state that he does not know the answer and ask for a volunteer to give a brief answer, brief because the question is only partially relevant
    D. tell the questioner that the question is not pertinent, show wherein it is not pertinent, and state that the time of the group should not be wasted on it

22. The one of the following circumstances when it would generally be MOST proper for a supervisor to do a job himself rather than to train a subordinate to do the job is when it is

    A. a job which the supervisor enjoys doing and does well
    B. not a very time-consuming job but an important one
    C. difficult to train another to do the job yet is not difficult for the supervisor to do
    D. unlikely that this or any similar job will have to be done again at any future time

23. Effective training of subordinates requires that the supervisor understand certain facts about learning and forgetting processes.
    Among these is the fact that people generally

    A. both learn and forget at a relatively constant rate and this rate is dependent upon their general intellectual capacity
    B. forget what they learned at a much greater rate during the first day than during subsequent periods
    C. learn at a relatively constant rate except for periods of assimilation when the quantity of retained learning decreases while information is becoming firmly fixed in the mind
    D. learn very slowly at first when introduced to a new topic, after which there is a great increase in the rate of learning

24. It has been suggested that a subordinate who likes his supervisor will tend to do better work than one who does not. According to the MOST widely-held current theories of supervision, this suggestion is a

    A. *bad one;* since personal relationships tend to interfere with proper professional relationships
    B. *bad one;* since the strongest motivating factors are fear and uncertainty
    C. *good one;* since liking one's supervisor is a motivating factor for good work performance
    D. *good one;* since liking one's supervisor is the most important factor in employee performance

25. A supervisor is supervising an employee who is very soon to complete his six months' probationary period. The supervisor finds him to be slow, to make many errors, to do work poorly, to be antagonistic toward the supervisor, and to be disliked by most of his co-workers. The supervisor is aware that he is the sole support of his wife and two children. He has never been late or absent during his service with the department. If he is terminated, there will be a considerable delay before a replacement for him arrives.
It would generally be BEST for the supervisor to recommend that this employee be

    A. transferred to work with another supervisor and other staff members with whom he may get along better
    B. retained but be very closely supervised until his work shows marked improvement
    C. retained since his services are needed with the expectation that he be terminated at some later date when a replacement is readily available
    D. terminated

KEY (CORRECT ANSWERS)

1. A
2. B
3. C
4. C
5. B

6. D
7. C
8. B
9. C
10. A

11. B
12. D
13. D
14. A
15. D

16. C
17. B
18. A
19. D
20. D

21. C
22. D
23. B
24. C
25. D

PHILOSOPHY, PRINCIPLES, PRACTICES, AND TECHNICS
OF
SUPERVISION, ADMINISTRATION, MANAGEMENT, AND ORGANIZATION

TABLE OF CONTENTS

	Page
MEANING OF SUPERVISION	1
THE OLD AND THE NEW SUPERVISION	1
THE EIGHT (8) BASIC PRINCIPLES OF THE NEW SUPERVISION	1
I. Principle of Responsibility	1
II. Principle of Authority	2
III. Principle of Self-Growth	2
IV. Principle of Individual Worth	2
V. Principle of Creative Leadership	2
VI. Principle of Success and Failure	2
VII. Principle of Science	3
VIII. Principle of Cooperation	3
WHAT IS ADMINISTRATION?	3
I. Practices Commonly Classed as "Supervisory"	3
II. Practices Commonly Classed as "Administrative"	3
III. Practices Commonly Classed as Both "Supervisory" and "Administrative"	4
RESPONSIBILITIES OF THE SUPERVISOR	4
COMPETENCIES OF THE SUPERVISOR	4
THE PROFESSIONAL SUPERVISOR-EMPLOYEE RELATIONSHIP	4
MINI-TEXT IN SUPERVISION, ADMINISTRATION, MANAGEMENT, AND ORGANIZATION	5
I. Brief Highlights	5
A. Levels of Management	6
B. What the Supervisor Must Learn	6
C. A Definition of Supervision	6
D. Elements of the Team Concept	6
E. Principles of Organization	6
F. The Four Important Parts of Every Job	7
G. Principles of Delegation	7
H. Principles of Effective Communications	7
I. Principles of Work Improvement	7
J. Areas of Job Improvement	7
K. Seven Key Points in Making Improvements	8

	L.	Corrective Techniques for Job Improvement	8
	M.	A Planning Checklist	8
	N.	Five Characteristics of Good Directions	9
	O.	Types of Directions	9
	P.	Controls	9
	Q.	Orienting the New Employee	9
	R.	Checklist for Orienting New Employees	9
	S.	Principles of Learning	10
	T.	Causes of Poor Performance	10
	U.	Four Major Steps in On-the-Job Instructions	10
	V.	Employees Want Five Things	10
	W.	Some Don'ts in Regard to Praise	11
	X.	How to Gain Your Workers' Confidence	11
	Y.	Sources of Employee Problems	11
	Z.	The Supervisor's Key to Discipline	11
	AA.	Five Important Processes of Management	12
	BB.	When the Supervisor Fails to Plan	12
	CC.	Fourteen General Principles of Management	12
	DD.	Change	12
II.	Brief Topical Summaries		13
	A.	Who/What is the Supervisor?	13
	B.	The Sociology of Work	13
	C.	Principles and Practices of Supervision	14
	D.	Dynamic Leadership	14
	E.	Processes for Solving Problems	15
	F.	Training for Results	15
	G.	Health, Safety, and Accident Prevention	16
	H.	Equal Employment Opportunity	16
	I.	Improving Communications	16
	J.	Self-Development	17
	K.	Teaching and Training	17
		1. The Teaching Process	17
		a. Preparation	17
		b. Presentation	18
		c. Summary	18
		d. Application	18
		e. Evaluation	18
		2. Teaching Methods	18
		a. Lecture	18
		b. Discussion	18
		c. Demonstration	19
		d. Performance	19
		e. Which Method to Use	19

PHILOSOPHY, PRINCIPLES, PRACTICES, AND TECHNICS
OF
SUPERVISION, ADMINISTRATION, MANAGEMENT, AND ORGANIZATION

MEANING OF SUPERVISION

The extension of the democratic philosophy has been accompanied by an extension in the scope of supervision. Modern leaders and supervisors no longer think of supervision in the narrow sense of being confined chiefly to visiting employees, supplying materials, or rating the staff. They regard supervision as being intimately related to all the concerned agencies of society, they speak of the supervisor's function in terms of "growth," rather than the "improvement" of employees.

This modern concept of supervision may be defined as follows: Supervision is leadership and the development of leadership within groups which are cooperatively engaged in inspection, research, training, guidance, and evaluation.

THE OLD AND THE NEW SUPERVISION

TRADITIONAL
1. Inspection
2. Focused on the employee
3. Visitation
4. Random and haphazard
5. Imposed and authoritarian
6. One person usually

MODERN
1. Study and analysis
2. Focused on aims, materials, methods, supervisors, employees, environment
3. Demonstrations, intervisitation, workshops, directed reading, bulletins, etc.
4. Definitely organized and planned (scientific)
5. Cooperative and democratic
6. Many persons involved (creative)

THE EIGHT (8) BASIC PRINCIPLES OF THE NEW SUPERVISION

I. Principle of Responsibility
   Authority to act and responsibility for acting must be joined.
   A. If you give responsibility, give authority.
   B. Define employee duties clearly.
   C. Protect employees from criticism by others.
   D. Recognize the rights as well as obligations of employees.
   E. Achieve the aims of a democratic society insofar as it is possible within the area of your work.
   F. Establish a situation favorable to training and learning.
   G. Accept ultimate responsibility for everything done in your section, unit, office, division, department.
   H. Good administration and good supervision are inseparable.

II. Principle of Authority
The success of the supervisor is measured by the extent to which the power of authority is not used.
   A. Exercise simplicity and informality in supervision
   B. Use the simplest machinery of supervision
   C. If it is good for the organization as a whole, it is probably justified.
   D. Seldom be arbitrary or authoritative.
   E. Do not base your work on the power of position or of personality.
   F. Permit and encourage the free expression of opinions.

III. Principle of Self-Growth
The success of the supervisor is measured by the extent to which, and the speed with which, he is no longer needed.
   A. Base criticism on principles, not on specifics.
   B. Point out higher activities to employees.
   C. Train for self-thinking by employees to meet new situations.
   D. Stimulate initiative, self-reliance, and individual responsibility
   E. Concentrate on stimulating the growth of employees rather than on removing defects.

IV. Principle of Individual Worth
Respect for the individual is a paramount consideration in supervision.
   A. Be human and sympathetic in dealing with employees.
   B. Don't nag about things to be done.
   C. Recognize the individual differences among employees and seek opportunities to permit best expression of each personality.

V. Principle of Creative Leadership
The best supervision is that which is not apparent to the employee.
   A. Stimulate, don't drive employees to creative action.
   B. Emphasize doing good things.
   C. Encourage employees to do what they do best.
   D. Do not be too greatly concerned with details of subject or method.
   E. Do not be concerned exclusively with immediate problems and activities.
   F. Reveal higher activities and make them both desired and maximally possible.
   G. Determine procedures in the light of each situation but see that these are derived from a sound basic philosophy.
   H. Aid, inspire, and lead so as to liberate the creative spirit latent in all good employees.

VI. Principle of Success and Failure
There are no unsuccessful employees, only unsuccessful supervisors who have failed to give proper leadership.
   A. Adapt suggestions to the capacities, attitudes, and prejudices of employees.
   B. Be gradual, be progressive, be persistent.
   C. Help the employee find the general principle; have the employee apply his own problem to the general principle.
   D. Give adequate appreciation for good work and honest effort.
   E. Anticipate employee difficulties and help to prevent them.
   F. Encourage employees to do the desirable things they will do anyway.
   G. Judge your supervision by the results it secures.

VII. Principle of Science
Successful supervision is scientific, objective, and experimental. It is based on facts, not on prejudices.
   A. Be cumulative in results.
   B. Never divorce your suggestions from the goals of training.
   C. Don't be impatient of results.
   D. Keep all matters on a professional, not a personal, level.
   E. Do not be concerned exclusively with immediate problems and activities.
   F. Use objective means of determining achievement and rating where possible.

VIII. Principle of Cooperation
Supervision is a cooperative enterprise between supervisor and employee.
   A. Begin with conditions as they are.
   B. Ask opinions of all involved when formulating policies.
   C. Organization is as good as its weakest link.
   D. Let employees help to determine policies and department programs.
   E. Be approachable and accessible—physically and mentally.
   F. Develop pleasant social relationships.

WHAT IS ADMINISTRATION

Administration is concerned with providing the environment, the material facilities, and the operational procedures that will promote the maximum growth and development of supervisors and employees. (Organization is an aspect and a concomitant of administration.)

There is no sharp line of demarcation between supervision and administration; these functions are intimately interrelated and, often, overlapping. They are complementary activities.

I. Practices Commonly Classed as "Supervisory"
   A. Conducting employees' conferences
   B. Visiting sections, units, offices, divisions, departments
   C. Arranging for demonstrations
   D. Examining plans
   E. Suggesting professional reading
   F. Interpreting bulletins
   G. Recommending in-service training courses
   H. Encouraging experimentation
   I. Appraising employee morale
   J. Providing for intervisitation

II. Practices Commonly Classified as "Administrative"
   A. Management of the office
   B. Arrangement of schedules for extra duties
   C. Assignment of rooms or areas
   D. Distribution of supplies
   E. Keeping records and reports
   F. Care of audio-visual materials
   G. Keeping inventory records
   H. Checking record cards and books

      I. Programming special activities
      J. Checking on the attendance and punctuality of employees

III. Practices Commonly Classified as Both "Supervisory" and "Administrative"
    A. Program construction
    B. Testing or evaluating outcomes
    C. Personnel accounting
    D. Ordering instructional materials

RESPONSIBILITIES OF THE SUPERVISOR

A person employed in a supervisory capacity must constantly be able to improve his own efficiency and ability. He represent the employer to the employees and only continuous self-examination can make him a capable supervisor.

Leadership and training are the supervisor's responsibility. An efficient working unit is one in which the employees work with the supervisor. It is his job to bring out the best in his employees. He must always be relaxed, courteous, and calm in his association with his employees. Their feelings are important, and a harsh attitude does not develop the most efficient employees.

COMPETENCES OF THE SUPERVISOR

    I. Complete knowledge of the duties and responsibilities of his position.
    II. To be able to organize a job, plan ahead, and carry through.
    III. To have self-confidence and initiative.
    IV. To be able to handle the unexpected situation and make quick decisions.
    V. To be able to properly train subordinates in the positions they are best suited for.
    VI. To be able to keep good human relations among his subordinates.
    VII. To be able to keep good human relations between his subordinates and himself and to earn their respect and trust.

THE PROFESSIONAL SUPERVISOR-EMPLOYEE RELATIONSHIP

There are two kinds of efficiency: one kind is only apparent and is produced in organizations through the exercise of mere discipline; this is but a simulation of the second, or true, efficiency which springs from spontaneous cooperation. If you are a manager, no matter how great or small your responsibility, it is your job, in the final analysis, to create and develop this involuntary cooperation among the people whom you supervise. For, no matter how powerful a combination of money, machines, and materials a company may have, this is a dead and sterile thing without a team of willing, thinking, and articulate people to guide it.

The following 21 points are presented as indicative of the exemplary basic relationship that should exist between supervisor and employee:

1. Each person wants to be liked and respected by his fellow employee and wants to be treated with consideration and respect by his superior.
2. The most competent employee will make an error. However, in a unit where good relations exist between the supervisor and his employees, tenseness and fear do not exist. Thus, errors are not hidden or covered up, and the efficiency of a unit is not impaired.

3. Subordinates resent rules, regulations, or orders that are unreasonable or unexplained.
4. Subordinates are quick to resent unfairness, harshness, injustices, and favoritism.
5. An employee will accept responsibility if he knows that he will be complimented for a job well done, and not too harshly chastised for failure; that his supervisor will check the cause of the failure, and, if it was the supervisor's fault, he will assume the blame therefore. If it was the employee's fault, his supervisor will explain the correct method or means of handling the responsibility.
6. An employee wants to receive credit for a suggestion he has made, that is used. If a suggestion cannot be used, the employee is entitled to an explanation. The supervisor should not say "no" and close the subject.
7. Fear and worry slow up a worker's ability. Poor working environment can impair his physical and mental health. A good supervisor avoids forceful methods, threats, and arguments to get a job done.
8. A forceful supervisor is able to train his employees individually and as a team, and is able to motivate them in the proper channels.
9. A mature supervisor is able to properly evaluate his subordinates and to keep them happy and satisfied.
10. A sensitive supervisor will never patronize his subordinates.
11. A worthy supervisor will respect his employees' confidences.
12. Definite and clear-cut responsibilities should be assigned to each executive.
13. Responsibility should always be coupled with corresponding authority.
14. No change should be made in the scope or responsibilities of a position without a definite understanding to that effect on the part of all persons concerned.
15. No executive or employee, occupying a single position in the organization, should be subject to definite orders from more than one source.
16. Orders should never be given to subordinates over the head of a responsible executive. Rather than do this, the officer in question should be supplanted.
17. Criticisms of subordinates should, whoever possible, be made privately, and in no case should a subordinate be criticized in the presence of executives or employees of equal or lower rank.
18. No dispute or difference between executives or employees as to authority or responsibilities should be considered too trivial for prompt and careful adjudication.
19. Promotions, wage changes, and disciplinary action should always be approved by the executive immediately superior to the one directly responsible.
20. No executive or employee should ever be required, or expected, to be at the same time an assistant to, and critic of, another.
21. Any executive whose work is subject to regular inspection should, wherever practicable, be given the assistance and facilities necessary to enable him to maintain an independent check of the quality of his work.

MINI-TEXT IN SUPERVISION, ADMINISTRATION, MANAGEMENT, AND ORGANIZATION

I. Brief Highlights

Listed concisely and sequentially are major headings and important data in the field for quick recall and review.

A. Levels of Management
Any organization of some size has several levels of management. In terms of a ladder, the levels are:

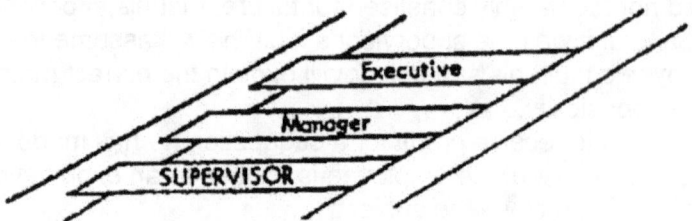

The first level is very important because it is the beginning point of management leadership.

B. What the Supervisor Must Learn
A supervisor must learn to:
1. Deal with people and their differences
2. Get the job done through people
3. Recognize the problems when they exist
4. Overcome obstacles to good performance
5. Evaluate the performance of people
6. Check his own performance in terms of accomplishment

C. A Definition of Supervisor
The term supervisor means any individual having authority, in the interests of the employer, to hire, transfer, suspend, lay-off, recall, promote, discharge, assign, reward, or discipline other employees or responsibility to direct them, or to adjust their grievances, or effectively to recommend such action, if, in connection with the foregoing, exercise of such authority is not of a merely routine or clerical nature but requires the use of independent judgment.

D. Elements of the Team Concept
What is involved in teamwork? The component parts are:
1. Members
2. A leader
3. Goals
4. Plans
5. Cooperation
6. Spirit

E. Principles of Organization
1. A team member must know what his job is.
2. Be sure that the nature and scope of a job are understood.
3. Authority and responsibility should be carefully spelled out.
4. A supervisor should be permitted to make the maximum number of decisions affecting his employees.
5. Employees should report to only one supervisor.
6. A supervisor should direct only as many employees as he can handle effectively.
7. An organization plan should be flexible.

8. Inspection and performance of work should be separate.
9. Organizational problems should receive immediate attention.
10. Assign work in line with ability and experience.

F. The Four Important Parts of Every Job
1. Inherent in every job is the *accountability* for results.
2. A second set of factors in every job is *responsibilities*.
3. Along with duties and responsibilities one must have the *authority* to act within certain limits without obtaining permission to proceed.
4. No job exists in a vacuum. The supervisor is surrounded by key *relationships*.

G. Principles of Delegation
Where work is delegated for the first time, the supervisor should think in terms of these questions:
1. Who is best qualified to do this?
2. Can an employee improve his abilities by doing this?
3. How long should an employee spend on this?
4. Are there any special problems for which he will need guidance?
5. How broad a delegation can I make?

H. Principles of Effective Communications
1. Determine the media.
2. To whom directed?
3. Identification and source authority.
4. Is communication understood?

I. Principles of Work Improvement
1. Most people usually do only the work which is assigned to them.
2. Workers are likely to fit assigned work into the time available to perform it.
3. A good workload usually stimulates output.
4. People usually do their best work when they know that results will be reviewed or inspected.
5. Employees usually feel that someone else is responsible for conditions of work, workplace layout, job methods, type of tools/equipment, and other such factors.
6. Employees are usually defensive about their job security.
7. Employees have natural resistance to change.
8. Employees can support or destroy a supervisor.
9. A supervisor usually earns the respect of his people through his personal example of diligence and efficiency.

J. Areas of Job Improvement
The areas of job improvement are quite numerous, but the most common ones which a supervisor can identify and utilize are:
1. Departmental layout
2. Flow of work
3. Workplace layout
4. Utilization of manpower
5. Work methods
6. Materials handling

7. Utilization
8. Motion economy

K. Seven Key Points in Making Improvements
1. Select the job to be improved
2. Study how it is being done now
3. Question the present method
4. Determine actions to be taken
5. Chart proposed method
6. Get approval and apply
7. Solicit worker participation

l. Corrective Techniques of Job Improvement
Specific Problems
1. Size of workload
2. Inability to meet schedules
3. Strain and fatigue
4. Improper use of men and skills
5. Waste, poor quality, unsafe conditions
6. Bottleneck conditions that hinder output
7. Poor utilization of equipment and machine
8. Efficiency and productivity of labor

General Improvement
1. Departmental layout
2. Flow of work
3. Work plan layout
4. Utilization of manpower
5. Work methods
6. Materials handling
7. Utilization of equipment
8. Motion economy

Corrective Techniques
1. Study with scale model
2. Flow chart study
3. Motion analysis
4. Comparison of units produced to standard allowance
5. Methods analysis
6. Flow chart and equipment study
7. Down time vs. running time
8. Motion analysis

M. A Planning Checklist
1. Objectives
2. Controls
3. Delegations
4. Communications
5. Resources
6. Manpower

7. Equipment
8. Supplies and materials
9. Utilization of time
10. Safety
11. Money
12. Work
13. Timing of improvements

N. Five Characteristics of Good Directions
In order to get results, directions must be:
1. Possible of accomplishment
2. Agreeable with worker interests
3. Related to mission
4. Planned and complete
5. Unmistakably clear

O. Types of Directions
1. Demands or direct orders
2. Requests
3. Suggestion or implication
4. volunteering

P. Controls
A typical listing of the overall areas in which the supervisor should establish controls might be:
1. Manpower
2. Materials
3. Quality of work
4. Quantity of work
5. Time
6. Space
7. Money
8. Methods

Q. Orienting the New Employee
1. Prepare for him
2. Welcome the new employee
3. Orientation for the job
4. Follow-up

R. Checklist for Orienting New Employees   Yes   No
1. Do you appreciate the feelings of new employees
   when they first report for work?   ___   ___
2. Are you aware of the fact that the new employee must
   make a big adjustment to his job?   ___   ___
3. Have you given him good reasons for liking the job and
   the organization?   ___   ___
4. Have you prepared for his first day on the job?   ___   ___
5. Did you welcome him cordially and make him feel needed?   ___   ___

	Yes	No

6. Did you establish rapport with him so that he feels free to talk and discuss matters with you? ___ ___
7. Did you explain his job to him and his relationship to you? ___ ___
8. Does he know that his work will be evaluated periodically on a basis that is fair and objective? ___ ___
9. Did you introduce him to his fellow workers in such a way that they are likely to accept him? ___ ___
10. Does he know what employee benefits he will receive? ___ ___
11. Does he understand the importance of being on the job and what to do if he must leave his duty station? ___ ___
12. Has he been impressed with the importance of accident prevention and safe practice? ___ ___
13. Does he generally know his way around the department? ___ ___
14. Is he under the guidance of a sponsor who will teach the right way of doing things? ___ ___
15. Do you plan to follow-up so that he will continue to adjust successfully to his job? ___ ___

S. Principles of Learning
1. Motivation
2. Demonstration or explanation
3. Practice

T. Causes of Poor Performance
1. Improper training for job
2. Wrong tools
3. Inadequate directions
4. Lack of supervisory follow-up
5. Poor communications
6. Lack of standards of performance
7. Wrong work habits
8. Low morale
9. Other

U. Four Major Steps in On-The-Job Instruction
1. Prepare the worker
2. Present the operation
3. Tryout performance
4. Follow-up

V. Employees Want Five Things
1. Security
2. Opportunity
3. Recognition
4. Inclusion
5. Expression

W. Some Don'ts in Regard to Praise
1. Don't praise a person for something he hasn't done.
2. Don't praise a person unless you can be sincere.
3. Don't be sparing in praise just because your superior withholds it from you.
4. Don't let too much time elapse between good performance and recognition of it

X. How to Gain Your Workers' Confidence
Methods of developing confidence include such things as:
1. Knowing the interests, habits, hobbies of employees
2. Admitting your own inadequacies
3. Sharing and telling of confidence in others
4. Supporting people when they are in trouble
5. Delegating matters that can be well handled
6. Being frank and straightforward about problems and working conditions
7. Encouraging others to bring their problems to you
8. Taking action on problems which impede worker progress

Y. Sources of Employee Problems
On-the-job causes might be such things as:
1. A feeling that favoritism is exercised in assignments
2. Assignment of overtime
3. An undue amount of supervision
4. Changing methods or systems
5. Stealing of ideas or trade secrets
6. Lack of interest in job
7. Threat of reduction in force
8. Ignorance or lack of communications
9. Poor equipment
10. Lack of knowing how supervisor feels toward employee
11. Shift assignments

Off-the-job problems might have to do with:
1. Health
2. Finances
3. Housing
4. Family

Z. The Supervisor's Key to Discipline
There are several key points about discipline which the supervisor should keep in mind:
1. Job discipline is one of the disciplines of life and is directed by the supervisor.
2. It is more important to correct an employee fault than to fix blame for it.
3. Employee performance is affected by problems both on the job and off.
4. Sudden or abrupt changes in behavior can be indications of important employee problems.
5. Problems should be dealt with as soon as possible after they are identified.
6. The attitude of the supervisor may have more to do with solving problems than the techniques of problem solving.
7. Correction of employee behavior should be resorted to only after the supervisor is sure that training or counseling will not be helpful.

8. Be sure to document your disciplinary actions.
9. Make sure that you are disciplining on the basis of facts rather than personal feelings.
10. Take each disciplinary step in order, being careful not to make snap judgments, or decisions based on impatience.

AA. Five Important Processes of Management
1. Planning
2. Organizing
3. Scheduling
4. Controlling
5. Motivating

BB. When the Supervisor Fails to Plan
1. Supervisor creates impression of not knowing his job
2. May lead to excessive overtime
3. Job runs itself—supervisor lacks control
4. Deadlines and appointments missed
5. Parts of the work go undone
6. Work interrupted by emergencies
7. Sets a bad example
8. Uneven workload creates peaks and valleys
9. Too much time on minor details at expense of more important tasks

CC. Fourteen General Principles of Management
1. Division of work
2. Authority and responsibility
3. Discipline
4. Unity of command
5. Unity of direction
6. Subordination of individual interest to general interest
7. Remuneration of personnel
8. Centralization
9. Scalar chain
10. Order
11. Equity
12. Stability of tenure of personnel
13. Initiative
14. Esprit de corps

DD. Change

Bringing about change is perhaps attempted more often, and yet less well understood, than anything else the supervisor does. How do people generally react to change? (People tend to resist change that is imposed upon them by other individuals or circumstances.

Change is characteristic of every situation. It is a part of every real endeavor where the efforts of people are concerned.

1. Why do people resist change?
   People may resist change because of:
   a. Fear of the unknown
   b. Implied criticism
   c. Unpleasant experiences in the past
   d. Fear of loss of status
   e. Threat to the ego
   f. Fear of loss of economic stability

2. How can we best overcome the resistance to change?
   In initiating change, take these steps:
   a. Get ready to sell
   b. Identify sources of help
   c. Anticipate objections
   d. Sell benefits
   e. Listen in depth
   f. Follow up

II. Brief Topical Summaries

   A. Who/What is the Supervisor?
      1. The supervisor is often called the "highest level employee and the lowest level manager."
      2. A supervisor is a member of both management and the work group. He acts as a bridge between the two.
      3. Most problems in supervision are in the area of human relations, or people problems.
      4. Employees expect: Respect, opportunity to learn and to advance, and a sense of belonging, and so forth.
      5. Supervisors are responsible for directing people and organizing work. Planning is of paramount importance.
      6. A position description is a set of duties and responsibilities inherent to a given position.
      7. It is important to keep the position description up-to-date and to provide each employee with his own copy.

   B. The Sociology of Work
      1. People are alike in many ways; however, each individual is unique.
      2. The supervisor is challenged in getting to know employee differences. Acquiring skills in evaluating individuals is an asset.
      3. Maintaining meaningful working relationships in the organization is of great importance.
      4. The supervisor has an obligation to help individuals to develop to their fullest potential.
      5. Job rotation on a planned basis helps to build versatility and to maintain interest and enthusiasm in work groups.
      6. Cross training (job rotation) provides backup skills.

7. The supervisor can help reduce tension by maintaining a sense of humor, providing guidance to employees, and by making reasonable and timely decisions. Employees respond favorably to working under reasonably predictable circumstances.
8. Change is characteristic of all managerial behavior. The supervisor must adjust to changes in procedures, new methods, technological changes, and to a number of new and sometimes challenging situations.
9. To overcome the natural tendency for people to resist change, the supervisor should become more skillful in initiating change.

C. Principles and Practices of Supervision
1. Employees should be required to answer to only one superior.
2. A supervisor can effectively direct only a limited number of employees, depending upon the complexity, variety, and proximity of the jobs involved.
3. The organizational chart presents the organization in graphic form. It reflects lines of authority and responsibility as well as interrelationships of units within the organization.
4. Distribution of work can be improved through an analysis using the "Work Distribution Chart."
5. The "Work Distribution Chart" reflects the division of work within a unit in understandable form.
6. When related tasks are given to an employee, he has a better chance of increasing his skills through training.
7. The individual who is given the responsibility for tasks must also be given the appropriate authority to insure adequate results.
8. The supervisor should delegate repetitive, routine work. Preparation of recurring reports, maintaining leave and attendance records are some examples.
9. Good discipline is essential to good task performance. Discipline is reflected in the actions of employees on the job in the absence of supervision.
10. Disciplinary action may have to be taken when the positive aspects of discipline have failed. Reprimand, warning, and suspension are examples of disciplinary action.
11. If a situation calls for a reprimand, be sure it is deserved and remember it is to be done in private.

D. Dynamic Leadership
1. A style is a personal method or manner of exerting influence.
2. Authoritarian leaders often see themselves as the source of power and authority.
3. The democratic leader often perceives the group as the source of authority and power.
4. Supervisors tend to do better when using the pattern of leadership that is most natural for them.
5. Social scientists suggest that the effective supervisor use the leadership style that best fits the problem or circumstances involved.
6. All four styles—telling, selling, consulting, joining—have their place. Using one does not preclude using the other at another time.

7. The theory X point of view assumes that the average person dislikes work, will avoid it whenever possible, and must be coerced to achieve organizational objectives.
8. The theory Y point of view assumes that the average person considers work to be a natural as play, and, when the individual is committed, he requires little supervision or direction to accomplish desired objectives.
9. The leader's basic assumptions concerning human behavior and human nature affect his actions, decisions, and other managerial practices.
10. Dissatisfaction among employees is often present, but difficult to isolate. The supervisor should seek to weaken dissatisfaction by keeping promises, being sincere and considerate, keeping employees informed, and so forth.
11. Constructive suggestions should be encouraged during the natural progress of the work.

E. Processes for Solving Problems
1. People find their daily tasks more meaningful and satisfying when they can improve them.
2. The causes of problems, or the key factors, are often hidden in the background. Ability to solve problems often involves the ability to isolate them from their backgrounds. There is some substance to the cliché that some persons "can't see the forest for the trees."
3. New procedures are often developed from old ones. Problems should be broken down into manageable parts. New ideas can be adapted from old one.
4. People think differently in problem-solving situations. Using a logical, patterned approach is often useful. One approach found to be useful includes these steps:
   a. Define the problem
   b. Establish objectives
   c. Get the facts
   d. Weigh and decide
   e. Take action
   f. Evaluate action

F. Training for Results
1. Participants respond best when they feel training is important to them.
2. The supervisor has responsibility for the training and development of those who report to him.
3. When training is delegated to others, great care must be exercised to insure the trainer has knowledge, aptitude, and interest for his work as a trainer.
4. Training (learning) of some type goes on continually. The most successful supervisor makes certain the learning contributes in a productive manner to operational goals.
5. New employees are particularly susceptible to training. Older employees facing new job situations require specific training, as well as having need for development and growth opportunities.
6. Training needs require continuous monitoring.
7. The training officer of an agency is a professional with a responsibility to assist supervisors in solving training problems.

8. Many of the self-development steps important to the supervisor's own growth are equally important to the development of peers and subordinates. Knowledge of these is important when the supervisor consults with others on development and growth opportunities.

G. Health, Safety, and Accident Prevention
1. Management-minded supervisors take appropriate measures to assist employees in maintaining health and in assuring safe practices in the work environment.
2. Effective safety training and practices help to avoid injury and accidents.
3. Safety should be a management goal. All infractions of safety which are observed should be corrected without exception.
4. Employees' safety attitude, training and instruction, provision of safe tools and equipment, supervision, and leadership are considered highly important factors which contribute to safety and which can be influenced directly by supervisors.
5. When accidents do occur, they should be investigated promptly for very important reasons, including the fact that information which is gained can be used to prevent accidents in the future.

H. Equal Employment Opportunity
1. The supervisor should endeavor to treat all employees fairly, without regard to religion, race, sex, or national origin.
2. Groups tend to reflect the attitude of the leader. Prejudice can be detected even in very subtle form. Supervisors must strive to create a feeling of mutual respect and confidence in every employee.
3. Complete utilization of all human resources is a national goal. Equitable consideration should be accorded women in the work force, minority-group members, the physically and mentally handicapped, and the older employee. The important question is: "Who can do the job?"
4. Training opportunities, recognition for performance, overtime assignments, promotional opportunities, and all other personnel actions are to be handled on an equitable basis.

I. Improving Communications
1. Communications is achieving understanding between the sender and the receiver of a message. It also means sharing information—the creation of understanding.
2. Communication is basic to all human activity. Words are means of conveying meanings; however, real meanings are in people.
3. There are very practical differences in the effectiveness of one-way, impersonal, and two-way communications. Words spoken face-to-face are better understood. Telephone conversations are effective, but lack the rapport of person-to-person exchanges. The whole person communicates.
4. Cooperation and communication in an organization go hand in hand. When there is a mutual respect between people, spelling out rules and procedures for communicating is unnecessary.
5. There are several barriers to effective communications. These include failure to listen with respect and understanding, lack of skill in feedback, and misinterpreting the meanings of words used by the speaker. It is also common

practice to listen to what we want to hear, and tune out things we do not want to hear.
6. Communication is management's chief problem. The supervisor should accept the challenge to communicate more effectively and to improve interagency and intra-agency communications.
7. The supervisor may often plan for and conduct meetings. The planning phase is critical and may determine the success or the failure of a meeting.
8. Speaking before groups usually requires extra effort. Stage fright may never disappear completely, but it can be controlled.

J. Self-Development
1. Every employee is responsible for his own self-development.
2. Toastmaster and toastmistress clubs offer opportunities to improve skills in oral communications.
3. Planning for one's own self-development is of vital importance. Supervisors know their own strengths and limitations better than anyone else.
4. Many opportunities are open to aid the supervisor in his developmental efforts, including job assignments; training opportunities, both governmental and non-governmental—to include universities and professional conferences and seminars.
5. Programmed instruction offers a means of studying at one's own rate.
6. Where difficulties may arise from a supervisor's being away from his work for training, he may participate in televised home study or correspondence courses to meet his self-development needs.

K. Teaching and Training
1. The Teaching Process
Teaching is encouraging and guiding the learning activities of students toward established goals. In most cases this process consists of five steps: preparation, presentation, summarization, evaluation, and application.

   a. Preparation
   Preparation is two-fold in nature; that of the supervisor and the employee. Preparation by the supervisor is absolutely essential to success. He must know what, when, where, how, and whom he will teach. Some of the factors that should be considered are:
   1) The objectives
   2) The materials needed
   3) The methods to be used
   4) Employee participation
   5) Employee interest
   6) Training aids
   7) Evaluation
   8) Summarization

   Employee preparation consists in preparing the employee to receive the material. Probably the most important single factor in the preparation of the employee is arousing and maintaining his interest. He must know the objectives of the training, why he is there, how the material can be used, and its importance to him.

b. Presentation
In presentation, have a carefully designed plan and follow it. The plan should be accurate and complete, yet flexible enough to meet situations as they arise. The method of presentation will be determined by the particular situation and objectives.

c. Summary
A summary should be made at the end of every training unit and program. In addition, there may be internal summaries depending on the nature of the material being taught. The important thing is that the trainee must always be able to understand how each part of the new material relates to the whole.

d. Application
The supervisor must arrange work so the employee will be given a chance to apply new knowledge or skills while the material is still clear in his mind and interest is high. The trainee does not really know whether he has learned the material until he has been given a chance to apply it. If the material is not applied, it loses most of its value.

e. Evaluation
The purpose of all training is to promote learning. To determine whether the training has been a success or failure, the supervisor must evaluate this learning.
In the broadest sense, evaluation includes all the devices, methods, skills, and techniques used by the supervisor to keep himself and the employees informed as to their progress toward the objectives they are pursuing. The extent to which the employee has mastered the knowledge, skills, and abilities, or changed his attitudes, as determined by the program objectives, is the extent to which instruction has succeeded or failed.
Evaluation should not be confined to the end of the lesson, day, or program but should be used continuously. We shall note later the way this relates to the rest of the teaching process.

2. Teaching Methods
A teaching method is a pattern of identifiable student and instructor activity used in presenting training material.
All supervisors are faced with the problem of deciding which method should be used at a given time.

a. Lecture
The lecture is direct oral presentation of material by the supervisor. The present trend is to place less emphasis on the trainer's activity and more on that of the trainee.

b. Discussion
Teaching by discussion or conference involves using questions and other techniques to arouse interest and focus attention upon certain areas, and by doing so creating a learning situation. This can be one of the most

valuable methods because it gives the employees an opportunity to express their ideas and pool their knowledge.

    c. Demonstration
The demonstration is used to teach how something works or how to do something. It can be used to show a principle or what the results of a series of actions will be. A well-staged demonstration is particularly effective because it shows proper methods of performance in a realistic manner.

    d. Performance
Performance is one of the most fundamental of all learning techniques or teaching methods. The trainee may be able to tell how a specific operation should be performed but he cannot be sure he knows how to perform the operation until he has done so.
As with all methods, there are certain advantages and disadvantages to each method.

    e. Which Method to Use
Moreover, there are other methods and techniques of teaching. It is difficult to use any method without other methods entering into it. In any learning situation, a combination of methods is usually more effective than any one method alone.

Finally, evaluation must be integrated into the other aspects of the teaching-learning process.

It must be used in the motivation of the trainees; it must be used to assist in developing understanding during the training; and it must be related to employee application of the results of training.

This is distinctly the role of the supervisor.

www.ingramcontent.com/pod-product-compliance
Lightning Source LLC
Chambersburg PA
CBHW082207300426
44117CB00016B/2702